STONE

IN STAFFORDSHIRE

THE
HISTORY OF A MARKET TOWN

by

Norman A. Cope, B.A.

Printed by Keele Graphic Services

On behalf of Stone Historical and Civic Society I would like to thank Mrs. Ruth Cope, the widow of Norman, for allowing this book to be reprinted.

Having attended St. Michael's School where he was Headmaster, I knew Mr. Cope for a number of years and it is thanks to his enthusiasm for the history of Stone that has lead to my own interest.

As well as writing several books on Stone, Mr. Cope collected an extensive archive. This was methodically catalogued and cross-referenced. On his death Mrs. Cope presented the collection to the William Salt Library at Stafford, where it is extensively used by those undertaking research into the town's history.

I would also like to thank Society stalwart Helen Holmes for suggesting this re-print; Secretary Tim Alston for all his hard work and Keele Graphic Services.

I hope that you will enjoy this book as much as I have over the years since it was first published in 1972.

Philip Leason
Chairman
STONE HISTORICAL AND CIVIC SOCIETY

Title page illustration is of the 13th century Seal of Stone Priory.

The wording reads: "SIGILLUM ECCLESIE SANCTE .MARIE ET SANCTI W . . . . . . (M)ARTIRIS DE STANIS" (Seal of the Church of Saint Mary and Saint Wulfad the Martyr of Stone).

(see page 31)

It is reproduced by courtesy of the Trustees of the British Museum.

This story of the growth of Stone is based on research and the collecting of information over a period of forty years. From the mass of information which has resulted, my aim has been to extract a developing account of the institutions and communications, the local names and traditions which have meant so much through the centuries.

I hope that the result will fill a three-fold purpose: as a satisfying record of Stone for those families who have long associations with the town; as a source of interest and information for the many new families who have made Stone their home-town; and as a reliable guide and encouragement to students who wish to pursue further the study of local history.

In offering the book to lovers of my native town, I acknowledge the patient encouragement of my wife, whose final determination made publication possible. I acknowledge, too, the sympathetic understanding of my printers, who have been unsparing in their efforts to convert typescript, sketches and photographs into book form.

Norman A. Cope
Walton, STONE.

CONTENTS

With twenty-three pages of illustrations

Pen-and-ink drawings are by the author

STONE MARKET CHARTER
1251 A.D.

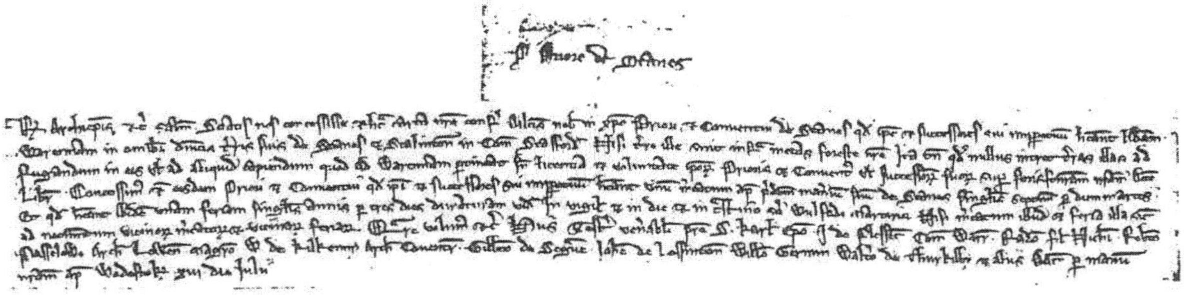

GRANTED TO THE PRIOR AND CONVENT OF STONE BY KING HENRY III.
AT WOODSTOCK, 13TH JULY 1251.

Public Record Office, London. Calendar of Charters, 35 Henry III. Close Rolls Henry III. 1247-1251, p 476.

1549 LICENCE TO ROBERT COLLYER

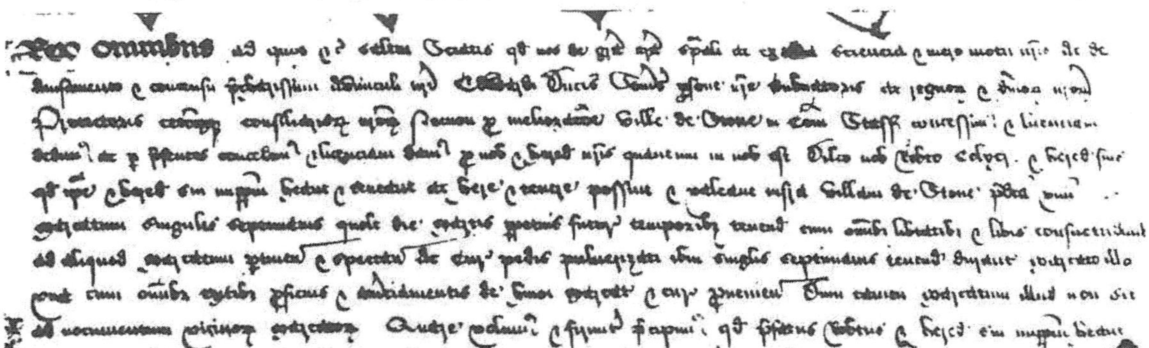

ENABLING HIM, AFTER THE DISSOLUTION OF THE PRIORY, TO MAINTAIN THE

PRIVILEGES GRANTED BY THE CHARTER OF 1251.

Patent Rolls (Chancery) 3 Edward VI., pt.1., m.16 (c.66/815/15) Public Record Office, London.

PLATE 1

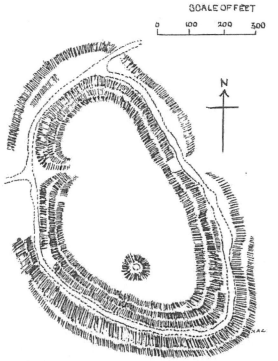

SCALE OF FEET

0   100   200   300

N

PLAN OF THE HILL FORT AT BURY BANK

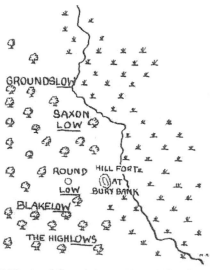

GROUNDSLOW

SAXON LOW

ROUND LOW   HILL FORT AT BURY BANK

BLAKELOW

THE HIGHLOWS

EARLY BRITISH PLACE-NAMES
"LOW" = burial-mound (A.S. hlāwe;
M.E. lawe, lowe

EARLY HISTORY

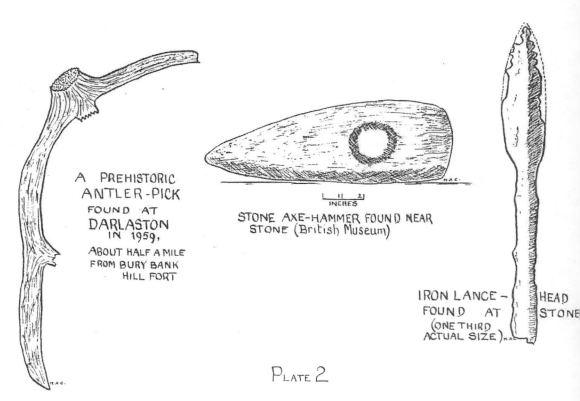

A PREHISTORIC ANTLER-PICK FOUND AT DARLASTON IN 1959, ABOUT HALF A MILE FROM BURY BANK HILL FORT

STONE AXE-HAMMER FOUND NEAR STONE (British Museum)

INCHES

IRON LANCE-HEAD FOUND AT STONE (ONE THIRD ACTUAL SIZE)

PLATE 2

CHAPTER 1

EARLIEST HISTORY

From the days even before recorded history we know something of the scattered folk who inhabited this area. The Trent Valley in the days of the earliest people was a wide swamp, and beyond the swamp the forests were vast and dangerous, with an almost impenetrable undergrowth. What was later to be known as the great Cank Forest stretched from the south of our present county to well northwards of *Stone*. The few inhabitants had, perforce, to keep mainly to the higher ground for their homes.

Life was a constant struggle to survive, to find the means to feed, and to protect themselves and their families. They were hunters who had to kill in order to live, who wore as clothes the skins of animals they had slain, and who ate, in their season, fruits and berries.

Their tools and weapons were simple, and made first of stone: axes, hammers and knives; fish-hooks were made of bone. Fish were plentiful in the river Trent, and in time dug-out canoes would make fishing easier. A fine specimen of an axe-hammer of this period, with a hole for the wooden handle, has been found in Stone.[1]

In the course of time there came from the continent men who were farmers rather than hunters, and who brought tools and weapons of bronze. Some form of religion was also practised, for they buried their dead in mounds, known as "barrows" or "lows",[2] and in these mounds stone and bronze implements have been found together. A leaf-shaped spear-head of bronze was found at Yarlet,[3] and fragments of urns of this period were discovered at *Saxon Low*, a conical hill about 40 feet high in *Tittensor Chase*[4] between Bury Bank Farm and Chase Lane.

In 1859 a small mound on Monument Hill at *Tittensor* was opened up. Beneath a layer of gravel a cavity was revealed, the two sides being formed by two good-sized slabs of stone, covered with a third slab. This cavity contained the burnt fragments of human bones, and immediately on top of the covering slab was found a flint arrowhead of crude workmanship, along with some flint chippings and fragments of pottery.[5]

During excavations at *Darlaston* in 1959 for a new road bridge a further relic of these early ages was dug up, 14 feet below the level of the river Trent's banks. This was a large antler, believed to have been used as a primitive type of pick, and the first discovery of its kind in Staffordshire.[6]

Most important of all our prehistoric relics is the *hill-fort at Bury Bank*. The lines of this ancient fort have been obscured by the planting of trees, but can still be followed without undue difficulty. The fort is in the shape of a rough ellipse, surrounded by steep slopes, designed for defence, and the ramparts are constructed of earth and rubble stone.[7] The area enclosed within the ramparts is 3½ acres. To the north-west there is a well-defined entrance, and some indications exist of a similar entrance in the opposite quarter.

In the southern part of the enclosure is a raised mound, remarkable because this is the only Staffordshire hill-fort with such a mound. Whether this mound was for military purposes, built to carry a wooden structure like the later Norman keeps[8] we shall never know. It may have been a place of burial. A rather unscientific excavation was made in 1860, and because "nothing was seen but a heap of stones, some bits of charcoal and some small fragments of bone",[9] the fragments were disregarded and valuable evidence lost.

In the days of its use by the early inhabitants, and again when the Saxons took possession of it, the ramparts would be surmounted by a stockade of tree trunks or wattling, or even a wall of dry stone work. In times of danger all the people of the district would leave their rude dwellings and seek protection, with their animals, inside the area of the fort. It was never merely the defended residence of a single household.

The people of this age lived simply, and changes were slow in Midland areas remote from the influence of the continent. Tools and weapons made of iron did eventually find their way to our district, and a leaf-shaped iron lance-head was found at the end of the 19th century, close to the National Westminster Bank in High St., 9½ feet below the surface of the ground, in gravel.[10]

Living mostly in hut villages, with fields crudely tilled, these people eked out an existence by agriculture and by the keeping of some livestock, augmented by hunting and fishing. Bones have been found in High St., and in Stafford St. of some of the animals they knew: the great ox ('bos primigenius') which ranged over Europe and which was contemporary with the mammoth and the woolly rhinoceros; the Celtic shorthorn cow ('bos longifrons') from which probably descended the small black cattle of the ancient Britons; and the horse, red deer, sheep and goat.

The impact of Roman civilisation was not felt until after 43 A.D. when the Emperor Claudius sent an expedition, for the landings of Julius Caesar a hundred years earlier had not been followed up. Conquest of the south of the country was not too difficult, but the process of Romanisation slowed down as the legions pushed northwards. In spite of the network of Roman roads, there is little proof that the Roman conquest and settlement of the upper Trent was at all complete.

A square entrenchment near *Hollywood*, in a coppice known as Campfield, is thought to be Roman, and there is an earthwork with double fosse near the *Hilderstone Brook*. A small bronze Roman coin was dug up here,[11] and at *Pirehill* a Roman hunting-spear was found. A wide-mouthed or bell-shaped urn of unglazed red clay[12] has been found at *Little Stoke*; it had incised lines in a zig-zag pattern and contained ashes and small pieces of human bones.

The Romans stayed in Britain until the beginning of the 5th century, when, struggling with invaders nearer home, they told the Britons that they no longer owed allegiance to the Emperor. Having relied on the Romans for so long, the Britons were unable to stand alone, and fell an easy prey to the invaders who soon began to enter our country.

Picts came swarming down from the north, and *Scots* from Ireland; from the continent came *Angles* and *Saxons*. These latter came as so many warlike bands, acting independently, save when common danger united them.

As before, the south was more easily conquered and settled; the invaders were slower to penetrate the forests, marshes and moorlands of the north. But, being men of the sea, the Angles and Saxons used the rivers as the surest approach to the heart of the country, and many pushed inland along the rivers that flow to the Humber.

The place-names in our district show the progress of the invaders up the Trent: *Weston, Aston, Stoke, Walton, Darlaston, Barlaston, Trentham*, the endings -ham, -tun, and -stok being early forms of 'home', 'township' and 'stockade'.

Of the two hundred years that followed the departure of the Romans we know little. It is certain, however, that these two 'lost' centuries were a period of confusion and warfare, during which the Romano-British civilisation and Christianity perished. The monk Gildas wrote that "the conflagration which started in the east did not stay its course until its ruddy tongue licked the western ocean."

The Anglo-Saxons buried their dead in the heathen way, on the top of hills or covered with mounds of earth or stones. One of these graves was opened at *Barlaston* in 1851.[13] It had been cut in solid rock on a slope of red sandstone, and in a north-south direction. The skeleton had disappeared, but other valuable remains were found. A cavity at the head of the grave contained a bronze bowl in which the head had apparently rested; on the right side was a long two-edged sword, and on the other side an iron dagger, characteristic of the Anglo-Saxon period. This bowl, an enamelled one, seriously injured by time, appears to have been very ornate, and was peculiar in being cast not wrought. Remains of no less than three bowls of similar character have been found in the neighbourhood of Dovedale.

These Anglo-Saxon invaders settled down as bands of kinsmen, led by their chief, and as the years passed they established their homesteads and gradually developed their civilisation. They built their rough timber houses, their byres and barns and enclosed them with an earthen wall and ditch, or took over existing hill-enclosures like that at *Bury Bank*. Immediately outside the ditch were the open fields which they had cleared, cut into strips or baulks, divided from each other by unploughed turf. Beyond the ploughland were the meadows on which all the flocks and herds of the village grazed in common, and beyond the meadows was a wide "mark" or "march", a belt of forest or fen. Any stranger who crossed this "mark" had first to blow a horn, or run the risk of being slain as an invader, for every stranger was regarded as a possible enemy.

In every village, or nearby, was a tree or mound at which the *Moot* or meeting was held, at which the freemen gathered to manage the affairs of the village. Here they settled village and farming matters, such as the crop rotation for the three-field system. The name *Motley Pits*, part of the Stone Common Plot, reminds us of this ancient system of government. Here the Moot assembled, and the very open fields with which, among others, the men concerned themselves, remained "open" until 1801. "Ley" is the old name for field or meadow, and occurs in *Tunley St.*, reminding us of the Town Ley. *Margaret St.*, on the edge of the old Stone Field, was long known as the *Green Baulk*.

Each village largely ruled itself, and a group of ten villages formed a "tithing". A group of a hundred villages formed a "hundred", and all cases, civil and criminal, were referred to the Hundred Moot. The *Stone district* forms part of the *Pirehill Hundred*, an area which exists to this day for licensing purposes. In later times a group of hundreds formed a shire.

Staffordshire must have been very thinly populated, for the county had only five hundreds,[14] whereas Kent had sixty-eight. The fact, too, that the Staffordshire hundreds are all named after some well-known and easily distinguished spot is further proof of the thin-ness of the population, and that the tenure of the newcomers was not too secure. *Pirehill* made an excellent rallying point in case of attack.

NOTES AND REFERENCES

1. Now in the British Museum. See the Victoria County History of Staffordshire, vol. I., p. 170. See plate 2 of this book.
2. See plate 2.
3. V.C.H. I., p. 179.
4. ibid., p. 180.
5. Staffordshire Advertiser, 29 December 1877.
6. Stone Guardian, 29 August 1959. See Plate 2.
7. V.C.H. I., pp. 341–343.
8. ibid.
9. Robert Garner: supplement to his Natural History of the County of Stafford.
10. V.C.H., I., pp. 179–180; and the Transactions of the North Staffordshire Field Club, vol. xxx., pp. 108–115. See plate 2.
11. V.C.H., I., p. 192.
12. Pitt: History of Staffordshire, I., 6; Stebbing Shaw: History of Staffordshire, I., 35.
13. North Staffordshire Field Club Transactions, vol. xl (1906), p. 148. The remains are now in the British Museum.
14. Offlow, Totmanslow, Pirehill, Seisdon and Cuttlestone.

CHAPTER 2

A MERCIAN KING AT BURY BANK

As time passed, the tribes who had settled in our country either conquered each other, or united for protection until there were *seven* petty English kingdoms. The invaders who had pushed furthest to the north-west became the men of the "*march*" or border, and their territory, known as *Mercia*, was the last of the English kingdoms to be formed, towards the close of the sixth century.

The first King of Mercia was said to be *Crida* (584–593), but the union of that extensive region was not completed until the accession of his grandson *Penda* (626–655), one of the greatest figures of early English history. By Penda's time the seven kingdoms were becoming reduced to three, Northumbria, *Mercia*, and Wessex gradually absorbing the rest. Northumbria, under its King Edwin, had been converted to Christianity by Paulinus; Augustine had brought the faith to Wessex in 597 A.D. Penda remained a follower of Woden, and this religious difference coincided with the struggle for supremacy between Mercia and Northumbria.

After the death of Penda at the battle of Winswaldfield in 655, his eldest son Peada succeeded as king. Peada was poisoned, after a reign of three years, by his wife Elflede. Peada was then succeeded, in 658 A.D., by his younger brother, *Wulfhere*, who is closely connected with *Stone*.

Wulfhere chose as one of his places of residence in this part of his kingdom the ancient hill-fort of *Bury Bank*. There is ample evidence to show that this enclosed settlement became known as *Wulfherecester*, or the castle of Wulfhere. One of the old Stone Priory documents records that "Robert de Suggenhall and Petronilla of Darlaston, daughter of Engenulf de Gresley, have given to the Prior and Convent of Stone one messuage in the manor of Darlaston, and all that part of the hill which is called Wulfecestre, which belongs to us."

Leland, the chronicler of Henry VIII's time, wrote: "Not veri far from Stone Priori appeareth the place where *King Woulpher's Castel or Manor Place* was. This *Byri Hill* stood on a rok by a broke side. There appere great dikes and squarid stones."[2]

Chetwynd's "History of Pirehill Hundred", written about the year 1680, records that "Within *Darlaston* on ye top of a rising ground ye marks of some fortifications are yet visible. The tradition is that here was once ye seat of Wulfhere, King of Mercia."[3]

Furthermore, Henry Bradshaw, who, in 1513, wrote the "Life of Saynt Werburga of Chester", recorded:

"This blessed lady and royall prynces,
Descendynge of noble and hye parentage,
Was daughter to Wulfer, the legend doth rehers,
Kynge of Merceland, and of famous lynage,

Her mother Ermenylde, ioned to hym in maryage:
They dwelled sometyme a lytell from Stone
At a place in Stafforde-shyre amyddes his regyon."[4]

The stones referred to by Leland have disappeared, but in 1879 Mr. William Molyneux stated that "there is a tradition that portions of the old farmhouse that stands at the foot of the hill were erected with timber and stones obtained from the ruins of the old 'castel'".

Like his father Penda, *Wulfhere* was at first a heathen, but when he sought in marriage Ermenilda, a saintly daughter of the royal house of Kent, he promised to become a Christian. His conversion was far from sincere, because Wulfhere reverted to his old beliefs almost immediately after he was married. Later he refused to allow his sons *Wulfad* and *Rufin* to be brought up anything but pagan. The daughter of the marriage, Werburga, was brought up to follow her mother's faith.

Legends[5] tell us that while the two princes were out hunting they met *Chad*, who had been sent to convert the savage Mercians. Both princes embraced the true faith, and paid frequent visits to the holy man. Meanwhile the beautiful Werburga was sought in marriage by one of her father's nobles, Werebode, also a pagan. Werburga refused, having vowed to devote her life to piety: this refusal had the support of her two brothers. This was too much for the cunning Werebode, who filled the King's mind with stories of plotting against him by the princes. In a fit of intense anger, Wulfhere is said to have slain both his sons; *Rufin* at Burston and *Wulfad* at *Stone*.

The King had no sooner returned to his home than Werebode was seized by sudden illness, and died miserably. Wulfhere himself was also ill, being overwhelmed with remorse, and the legend tells how the King eventually visited Chad to receive absolution at his hands, and how he proved by deed as well as by word his complete acceptance of the faith.

After the slaying of the princes, their broken-hearted mother had taken up their bodies and caused them to be buried together at the spot where Wulfad fell, beneath a great cairn of stones. From this act, Stone, or as it was in earliest times, Stanes, took its name. Writing in 1632, the historian Speed said:

"Their martyred bodies Queen Ermenild, their mother, caused to be buried in a sepulcher of stone, and thereupon a faire church to be erected, which by reason of the many stones thither brought for that purpose, *was ever after called Stones, and is now a Market Towne in the same county (of Stafford)*".[6]

Another version tells that:

"Upon this change the Christians, according to the custom of the Saxons, gathered stones, and heaped them up in the place where Wulfhere had slain his sons, to preserve the memory of the place; which remained some time. Queen Ermenild, their mother, turned them into a fair tomb enclosing their bodies, and thereon erected a fair church, with the stones brought thither at first, and many others which she caused to be brought, over their Tomb. After this church was built, and consecrated, a Town presently grew up, which the history of Peterborough tells us was called *Stone*, from the stones amassed together; Queen Ermenild is also said to have built a small Nunnery there."[7]

There is considerable evidence to show that Wulfhere did carry out his solemn promises to Chad. He rebuilt the church at *Eccleshall*, which he had destroyed shortly before; he founded the Abbey at Peterborough, and helped with the buildings at Stone. Henry Bradshaw wrote in 1513:

> "Also there was founded at Stone a pryorye
> In the honour of God and martyrs twayne."[8]

This small priory or hermitage was built about 670 A.D., and a *church* adjoining at the same date, dedicated to *St. Mary and St. Wulfad*. A deed of Robert de Stafford, dated about 1155 A.D., confirms grants of lands to the church of this name at *Stone*.[9] The Stone Chartulary, of slightly later date, contains transcripts of the deeds relating to the grants of rents in Stafford by Thomas, son of Brien of Eccleshale and others for the support of a lamp to burn perpetually before the high altar of Stone and the tomb of the Blessed Martyr Saint Wulfad.[10]

No date is known for the canonisation of the princes, but a hymn invoking Wulfad's protection has been found written on the fly-leaf of a manuscript in the Bodleian library, and experts are agreed that the hand-writing is of the 12th century. A translation of this hymn reads:

> "Hail, bruised stem of Mercia's kingly tree!
> Already is the pile prepared for thee.
> While sacrifice supreme is being made,
> On thee thy father draws his ruthless blade.
> Instead of Isaac, thou the lamb to kill,
> For this new Abraham who climbs the hill.
> Earth's pomp is dross; eternal glory thine.
> Guard us, and cherish us, Martyr divine."[11]

Finally, William Dugdale's "Monasticon" prints in full the tablet or 'Pedigree' which used to hang in the refectory of the priory; the origin of the foundation is again ascribed to Queen Ermenild in memory of her two sons, and in particular of Wulfad.[12]

Meanwhile, the Princess *Werburga*, after the tragic death of her brothers, had entered the Abbey of Ely as a nun. There, to quote Bradshaw's old verse account, she lived in prayer, penance and contemplation, "her body upon earth, her soul in heaven lent."

When Wulfhere died in 675, he was buried at Lichfield. His brother, *Ethelred*, succeeded him, and he made Werburga superintendent of all the religious houses in the kingdom. With his help she founded the house of *Trentham*, that of Hanbury near Tutbury, and of Weden in Northamptonshire.

Werburga resided mostly at Weden and Trentham, and many miracles are ascribed to her. When her end drew near, she visited all the places under her care, giving her last orders, including one that her body should be buried at Hanbury.

She died at Trentham on February 3rd. 699. Her body was brought to the church, which then adjoined the priory, and watch was kept over it. The sisters of Trentham wished to retain the body, but legend says that by some miracle the watchers fell asleep, and while they slept, the people of Hanbury came and took the body to that house in furtherance of Werburga's wish.

Her body was raised in 708, in the presence of King Coelred, his council and many bishops; it was found "entire and sweet-looking" and was enshrined at Hanbury on June 21st. There it remained for nearly 200 years, until the Danish invasions.

In 875, when the Danish fury swept over Mercia, and the intruders had advanced as far as Repton in Derbyshire, within five miles of Hanbury, the people, in fear, carried the shrine to Chester. Here it was received in the mother church of Peter and Paul. In later years a stately minster was built over the relics of St. Werburga, and became the present Chester Cathedral. A shrine which formerly contained the relics of Werburga can still be seen behind the high altar of the cathedral.

The Danes came the way of previous invaders, using the river valleys, and soon they had attacked Hanbury, Stone, Stafford, Tamworth and Lichfield.

Following the defeats of the Danes in 878 by King Alfred, and the division of the country, North Staffordshire would be in the Danelaw, but Danish settlements in this area were few and very weak. The Norse word 'car' and 'carr', meaning a marsh, is preserved in the name *Carr-house*, a mile and a half to the south-east of Stone.

Edward the Elder, succeeding Alfred, continued the struggle; his sister, Ethelfleda, did much to keep the Danes in check, and became known as the "Lady of Mercia". Indeed, when she died in 918, Staffordshire was practically free from Danes.

Further waves of Danes came in during the reign of Ethelred the Unready, and it was his foolishness which let loose the full fury of Danish savagery. He ordered a general massacre of Danes on St. Brice's Day in 1002. In Staffordshire a great massacre took place at Hound Hill, near Tutbury. During the avenging attacks, the Danes destroyed Eccleshall Church in 1010, and so damaged the little religious establishment at *Stone* that only a handful of nuns were able to struggle on until the Norman conquest.

NOTES AND REFERENCES

1. S.H.C. VI. Pt. I., p. 9.
2. John Leland: Itinerary in or about the year 1535–1543, ed. by Lucy Toulmin Smith.
3. S.H.C. XII. (N.S.) p. 100.
4. Henry Bradshaw: Life of Saynt Werburga of Chester, par. 98 (Early English Text Society, O.S.88).

5. For these legends see:
    (a) an account in a Peterborough book written about 970 A.D., and reproduced in Dugdale's "Monasticon", vol. VI. Pt. 1.
    (b) a tablet which hung in Stone Priory at the dissolution. (Dugdale: op. cit.)
    (c) Henry Bradshaw: op. cit.
    (d) Beresford: Memorials of Old Staffordshire, pp. 106–110.
    (e) Mark Hughes: Story of Staffordshire, pp. 34–37.
    (f) Hutchinson: The Archdeaconry of Stoke-on-Trent.
    (g) Rev. R. H. Warner: Life and Legends of St. Chad.
6. Speed: Historie of Great Britaine, 1632, p. 305.
7. Magna Britannia et Hibernia Antiqua et Nova, vol. V. in the Savoy, 1730.
8. Henry Bradshaw: op. cit.
9. "Ecclesiae Sanctae Mariae et Sancti Wlfadi de Stanes" (S.H.C. II. Pt. 1, pp. 236–7).
10. S.H.C. VI. Pt. 1, p. 28.
11. Bodley Ms. No. 343, printed in J. L. & Karl Cherry's "Historical Studies relating chiefly to Staffordshire." 1908, pp. 40–41.
12. Dugdale: op. cit.

CHAPTER 3

THE NORMAN CONQUEST

The victory at Hastings in 1066 was only the beginning of the Norman Conquest of England, and it was many years before William's hold on anything more than the southern districts was secure.

The greatest of the nobles who eventually came to Staffordshire was *Robert Tonei*, who, with his brother Nigel, had come over with the Conqueror. Both were liberally rewarded with land. They were, indeed, kinsmen of William, for their father was Richard, standard-bearer of Normandy, himself descended from Malahusius, uncle of Duke Rollo, the first Norseman to settle in Normandy.

Robert Tonei made Stafford his residence, and is subsequently known as *"de Stafford"*. Robert held no less than 150 lordships, of which more than half lay in Staffordshire. But these lordships were rarely adjoining each other, for William took the precaution of spreading them among a number of nobles, and retaining many himself.

When William had secured his position, he sent commissioners throughout the land to get particulars of every estate, and the results of their labours are preserved in the "Domesday Book". This survey shows how terribly the county of Stafford had suffered. It had always been thinly populated, for half the land recorded in the county was classed as woodland. Moreover, the county was still suffering from the effects of waves of destruction, first by the Danes before the Lady of Mercia recovered the county in 913, and secondly by Edmund Ironside in 1013. After the conquest, Staffordshire was seething with hatred of the Norman barons on whom the estates in the county were being bestowed, and in 1069 was in open revolt. William was ruthless in suppressing rebellion: with fire and sword he laid waste these districts which opposed him and instigated "the most terrible visitation that had ever fallen on any large part of England since the Danish wars of Alfred's time."[1]

It is no wonder that a large part of Staffordshire had to be described as "waste", not meaning the waste-land of moor and heath, but land which had lapsed out of cultivation; no wonder that "customary payments" were few, and that there were not many priests. The recorded population of the whole county in 1086 was about 3,000, a mere third of the present population of Stone.

In the *Stone* district King William held the "manors" or vills of *Trentham*, where there were 7½ plough-teams, 8 villeins, 7 cottagers, a bailiff and a priest; and *Sandon* with 10 plough-teams, 18 villeins, 8 cottagers and 7 acres of meadow. The King also held the waste vills of *Fulford, Mill Meece, Enson, Coton Hayes, Hilcote, Aston, Shelton-under-Harley,* and *Hatton;* one of the two holdings at each of *Cotwalton, Hilderstone* and *Milwich.* Although in all these waste vills there was total land for some fifteen ploughs, none is recorded, nor any population.

The *Abbey of St. Mary of Burton-on-Trent* was given the manor of *Darlaston,* now recovering from loss of production, and the *Church of Saint Remigius of Rheims*

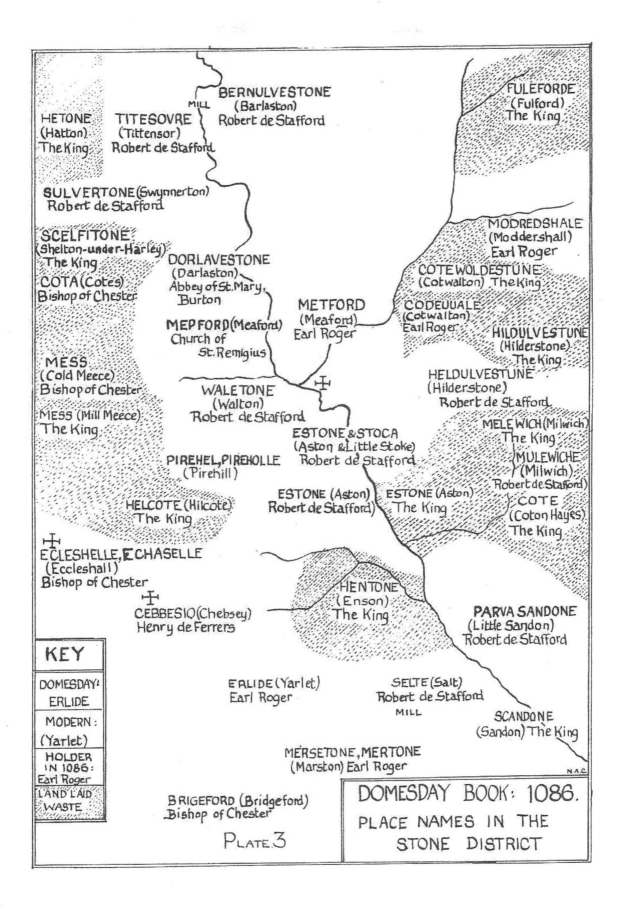

HETONE (Hatton) The King

TITESOVRE (Tittensor) Robert de Stafford

BERNULVESTONE (Barlaston) Robert de Stafford

MILL

FULEFORDE (Fulford) The King

SULVERTONE (Swynnerton) Robert de Stafford

SCELFITONE (Shelton-under-Harley) The King

COTA (Cotes) Bishop of Chester

DORLAVESTONE (Darlaston) Abbey of St. Mary, Burton

MODREDSHALE (Moddershall) Earl Roger

COTEWOLDESTUNE (Cotwalton) The King

MEPFORD (Meaford) Church of St. Remigius

METFORD (Meaford) Earl Roger

CODEUUALE (Cotwalton) Earl Roger

HILDULVESTUNE (Hilderstone) The King

MESS (Cold Meece) Bishop of Chester

WALETONE (Walton) Robert de Stafford

HELDULVESTUNE (Hilderstone) Robert de Stafford

MESS (Mill Meece) The King

ESTONE & STOCA (Aston & Little Stoke) Robert de Stafford

MELEWICH (Milwich) The King

MULEWICHE (Milwich) Robert de Stafford

PIREHEL, PIREHOLLE (Pirehill)

ESTONE (Aston) Robert de Stafford

ESTONE (Aston) The King

COTE (Coton Hayes) The King

HELCOTE (Hilcote) The King

ECLESHELLE, ECHASELLE (Eccleshall) Bishop of Chester

CEBBESIO (Chebsey) Henry de Ferrers

HENTONE (Enson) The King

PARVA SANDONE (Little Sandon) Robert de Stafford

ERLIDE (Yarlet) Earl Roger

SELTE (Salt) Robert de Stafford MILL

SCANDONE (Sandon) The King

MERSETONE, MERTONE (Marston) Earl Roger

BRIGEFORD (Bridgeford) Bishop of Chester

PLATE 3

N.A.C.

DOMESDAY BOOK: 1086.
PLACE NAMES IN THE STONE DISTRICT

held *Meaford*, with its three plough-teams, its wood and three acres of meadow. The abbey of Burton had been founded in 1002 by the great *Wulfric Spot* whose name is remembered in the Stone district by place-names such as *Spot Acre, Spot Gate,* and *Spot Grange.* There was said to be a hospice in the Spot area, to which travellers from Stone made their way by those ancient roads over the Red Hill and Cotwalton Drumble which remain as field paths to this day.

The *Bishop of Chester* held *Fradswell* and *Bridgeford*, as well as *Eccleshall*, which, with its twenty dependent holdings, was one of the largest composite manors in Staffordshire. The Bishop also had the vills of *Cotes* and *Cold Meece* which were waste.

Roger, Earl of Shrewsbury, who had fought at Hastings, held *Marston* and *Yarlet*, a part of *Meaford, Moddershall* and *one of the manors of Cotwalton*, which, unlike the King's holding, was under cultivation.

Henry de Ferrers, who had also fought at Hastings, and who was a Domesday commissioner, held the manor of *Chebsey.*

Robert de Stafford held *Walton*, now a part of Stone, *Aston and Little Stoke*, one of the holdings at *Hilderstone*, which was well stocked by comparison with the King's waste there; *Milwich, Tittensor* where there was a mill worth 8d., *Barlaston, Aston, Salt* which had a mill worth 3s., *Swynnerton* and *Little Sandon*. The distinction between Sandon (the King's) and Little Sandon is the only example of its kind in the Staffordshire Domesday.

The Parish of *Stone* is not mentioned by name, being formed of parts of a number of Domesday vills. The entry for *Walton* reads:

"Robert (de Stafford) holds Walton and Ernald holds it from him. There are III hides.[2] There is land for VI ploughs. In the demesne there is one, and VII villeins and II cottagers[3] and V slaves[4] with a priest who have IV ploughs. The wood is II furlongs long and I wide, and the pasture is of like extent. It is worth LX shillings. Achil a free man held it and gave I carucate[5] of this land to his sister.[6]"

The recording of this priest at Walton shows that *Stone* was included in that manor and confirms the establishment of the early church in Stone, remaining at the time of Domesday. Indeed, this is one of only ten places in North Staffordshire with a priest. There may even have been some nuns remaining. Tanner[7] notes that "some few nuns were apparently in possession of the place, survivors at the time of the Conquest of a former nunnery."

The *Stone district*, then, was really a series of manors held by the various lords, or by the King himself, with a church at what was in time to become the centre of a mediaeval town.

Marjorie and C. H. B. Quennell[8] have given us a picture of the Norman system of land tenure:

"The lord held his land from the King on this condition—he had to promise to help the King and be his man, and this same idea ran through the whole of the society of the time . . . Here are typical conditions on which the villein held his land from the lord. In the spring he had to plough 4 acres for his lord, and each villein supplied two oxen for the lord's plough-team for three days in the winter, three in the spring and one in summer. In addition he must work three days a week on the lord's land, or pay a yearly toll. He had to follow his lord to war, sit in his court of justice, and uphold customs which were to become laws. The terms of his holding were copied into the Court Roll, and so long as he rendered service in accordance with these, he could not be turned out. . . . The villein was in reality the backbone of the countryside, free on three days to work on his own land, owning cattle, and having the great interest of doing well or badly. In times of peace the village was like one large farm—the common fields were ploughed, harrowed, sown and reaped by the joint labours of all the villeins, and each of the latters' holdings consisted of a strip or strips in the open fields. The woods were used for feeding swine; the cattle grazed on the common land, and there were meadows for hay." Some of these features were to remain in the Stone district for centuries.

NOTES AND REFERENCES

1. F. M. Stenton: Anglo-Saxon England (Oxford 1943) p. 597.
2. A hide was a large and variable number of acres, usually about 120, and forming the unit of tax.
3. A cottager or small-holder was bound to the land like the villein, but was of lower rank.
4. Slave (serf); bound to work for his master.
5. A carucate was a measure of land, believed by Eyton to equal a hide.
6. H. M. Fraser: Staffordshire Domesday (Stone 1936) pp. 74–75.
7. Tanner: Notitia Monastica (Staffordshire xxv).
8. A History of Everday Things in England, part 1, pp. 47–49 (Batsford).

CHAPTER 4

THE AUGUSTINIAN PRIORY AT STONE

There is little doubt that at the time of the Norman conquest a church existed in what is now the town of Stone, served by the priest recorded in 1086 as living in the manor of Walton. It is very probable, too, that a few nuns were still clinging to the small nunnery founded by Queen Ermenild. Quite probably the carucate of land given by Achil, a Saxon free man, to his sister before the conquest, was in reality a gift to this religious community.

After the Normans had established themselves, *Stone Church* was in the gift or advowson of *Ernald*, who held from Robert de Stafford I the whole manor of Walton. And so it would have continued, but for two unexpected events. The first was the appearance on the scene of *Geoffrey de Clinton*, Henry I's chamberlain and treasurer. He had been granted the manor of Kenilworth by Henry I., and in 1122 he founded the Augustinian (or Austin) priory for black canons at Kenilworth. From that time he was always eager to acquire property which could be added to the endowment of Kenilworth Priory. It was for this reason that Geoffrey de Clinton obtained Stone Church from Ernald's son, *Enisan*. A deed (c. 1122–1125)[1] records his grant to Kenilworth Priory of "Stone Church which I obtained from Enisan, in whose demesne it is established, with the consent of Nicholas de Stafford, lord of the fee."

The second unexpected event was that a few years later Enisan's son, *Ernald*, committed a murder in or near Stone. The old mediaeval rhyming chronicle which hung in the priory at the dissolution relates that it was the murder of two nuns and a priest. The Pipe Roll of 1130 does not endorse this, but records that "Ernald, son of Enisan, owes 10 marks of silver that he may not be prosecuted for the death of some persons whom he had killed."[2]

With regard to this crime, two theories are possible. Either Geoffrey de Clinton took advantage of it to extort from the father, Enisan, more land on which to found a priory in Stone as a daughter-house to Kenilworth; or the father had to sell the land in order to raise the money to pay the fine. The fact that on the same Pipe Roll Liulph de Audley was fined 200 marks for homicide (compared with Ernald's 10 marks) strongly suggests that the crime was expiated with land.

The first actual mention of a daughter-house of Kenilworth at Stone is in a charter of 1138–1147, by which Robert de Stafford II granted "to the church of Stone and the canons serving God there" considerable spiritual and temporal property. It is possible that this is the foundation charter of Stone Priory, and that after the death of the powerful Clinton, Robert decided to give his support to this priory where his father Nicholas de Stafford had been buried (c. 1138). Robert's charter stressed his relationship to the priory as "Brother and patron of the same church at Stone" and expressed a desire to be buried there. Both Robert and his wife were buried in the cloister, near to the chapter-house door, and close to Robert's parents.

By this charter Robert de Stafford confirmed to the canons "my chapel of Stafford"[3], the churches of Madeley, of Tysoe (Warws.) and Wolford (Worcs.), and a mill at Wootton Wawen (Worcs.).

Spiritual endowments came quickly, but involved the Prior in considerable litigation. The *church of Milwich* was given by Nicholas de Milwich and confirmed by Robert de Stafford, though the title was not finally secured until 1233.

About 1155 Walter de Caverswall, with the consent of his overlord, gave his half share of the *church of Stoke-on-Trent*, but by the early 1220s the Earl of Chester challenged the Prior's entitlement, and the Priory had to surrender its share in return for two virgates of land in Seabridge (Stoke parish).

The priory claimed *Swynnerton church* but the claim was long resisted by the two clerks there. About 1187, however, with the assent of the lord of Swynnerton, the clerks conceded that their church was subject, as a parochial chapel, to Stone Priory, and agreed to pay to the "mother-church" an annual pension of £2.

Both the *church of Dilhorne* and the *church of Bradley* were confirmed to the Priory by Pope Alexander III. At about the same time certain rights in the *church of Checkley* were surrendered to Alice de Hopton in return for a rent of 20s. and the tithes of Normacott.

On the death of Robert de Stafford III in 1194, the Stafford properties passed to Hervey Bagot, who had married Robert's sister, Millicent. In 1226, when Hervey (now de Stafford) was taken ill at Tysoe in Warwickshire, the canons of Stone permitted him to have private services in his chamber there from Christmas to Epiphany, taken by Brother Peter, one of their number, but this concession was clearly only a temporary one. All the Augustinian canons, or black canons as they were called from the colour of their habits, were priests. The extent to which the Stone canons served their parish churches themselves, or by employing secular priests not belonging to their order, is uncertain. In 1259, however, a papal indult, after noting that the church of Stone was a parish church, and conventual, and had two secular priests appointed by the canons, allowed that they should not be compelled to establish a permanent secular priest there.

Hervey de Stafford made a general confirmation of grants to the Priory between 1217 and 1237. From this we learn that the Priory owned "half a virgate in the vill of *Darlaston;* a messuage in the vill; half an acre in Netherholm, part of the hill called *Wulfecestre* and part of the castell, six acres of the demesne and the land in Darlaston which is called *the Buri* which extends from the vill at Darlaston as far as the wood at Tittensor". The Priory also received from Ada de Beauchamp of Nantwich "ten acres of land in *Little Sandon*, and three cart-loads of wood weekly to be taken out of the woods there . . . for the health of her husband's soul, her own and her son Hugh's . . .&c."

When Hervey de Stafford died (c.1214) he was buried in the chapter-house, and in 1224 Millicent was laid beside him.

The canons never owned very much land outside the Stone district, but privileges and gifts from the Crown helped to augment their resources in the

13th century. On the 13th July 1251 at Woodstock, the Prior was granted a *market charter*[4] by King Henry III., which benefited the townspeople as well as the Priory. These are the main provisions:

"CHARTER

"*The King* to the Archbishops, Bishops . . . and his faithful people in *County Stafford* . . . .
Greeting. Know that we have granted and by this our *Charter* confirmed to our beloved in Christ the *Prior and Convent of Stone* that he and his successors for ever should have free Warren in all his demesne lands of *Stone* and *Stallington* in the County of Stafford. Unless these lands should be within the bounds of our forest . . . .

We grant also to them the Prior and Convent that they and their successors for ever should have *one market at the aforesaid manor of Stone weekly on Tuesdays.* And they should have *one fair* there each year *lasting three days,* namely on the vigil, on the feast day,[5] and on the morrow of St. Wulfad the Martyr, unless that market or that fair should be to the damage of neighbouring markets or neighbouring fairs. . . .

Given by our hand at *Woodstock, xiij day of July (1251)*"

The Prior paid 20 marks for this charter[6], and at a Stafford Assize in 1293 he produced it in order to prove his rights.[7]

In 1266 the King ordered 12 timber oaks to be sent to the priory from Cannock Forest, and in 1282 he granted the canons a buck from the forest.

The King exacted as well conferred favours. In 1315 *William de Blakelow,* who had fought at Bannockburn and in the last siege at Carlisle, where he was maimed, was sent to the Priory at Stone to receive maintenance for life.[8]

This was not the only drain on the Priory's resources. There were many casual callers requiring food and lodging, but much more costly were the nobles and visitors, often sent by the King, who claimed "corrody" or free "keep" during their stay.

In 1287 *Thomas de Milwich* failed to appear in court to prosecute his suit against the Prior. An agreement was afterwards made between them, by which Thomas gave up his claim to the corrody for which he sued, and the Prior acknowledged a debt to Thomas of 18 marks.[9]

In 1295 *John, Prior of Stone,* had to answer at the Assizes at Tamworth for refusing a corrody to *William de Cotes.* The corrody consisted of: "Every day a loaf of bread, a gallon of beer, a 'potagium' or pan of soup and 'ferculum' or dinner tray, as given to one of the canons; a robe annually to the value of a mark; sustenance for a horse in hay and oats for three nights, the oats amounting to a bushel; the corrody for a groom; four cartloads of wood annually, and two candles of tallow or wax every night from the Feast of All Saints till the Feast of the Purification of the Blessed Mary."[10]

It is not surprising that in 1343, when Stone sought leave to appropriate the church at Madeley, of which they had held the advowson since 1138, the Prior pleaded the great charges he was incurring for hospitality, owing to the Priory being *Juxta viam regiam* (on the King's highway).

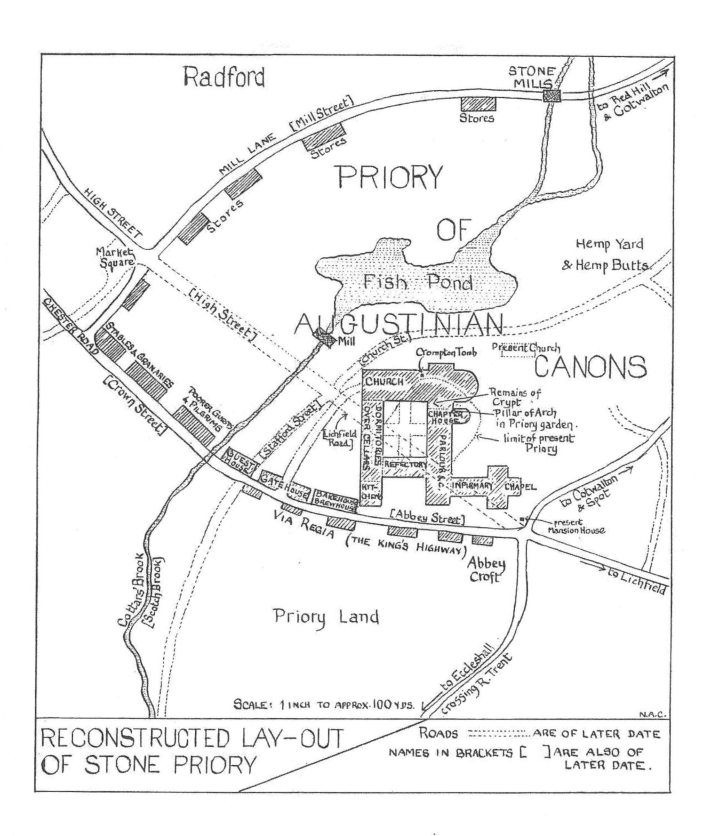

RECONSTRUCTED LAY-OUT OF STONE PRIORY

PLATE 4

The *King's highway* from south to north followed the line of Lichfield Rd. as far as the "Mansion House", then along Abbey St., Crown St. and Newcastle St. A road from Eccleshall crossed the river Trent by a ford (on the lower side of the present bridge) and later by a narrow pack-horse bridge, remains of which are incorporated, and visible, in the arches at the Stone end of the present structure; this road then crossed Westbridge Park to join Abbey St. near Abbey Croft and the "Mansion House" to continue through the Hempbutts to Red Hill and Cotwalton. Mill St. joined the main road to the Red Hill road, after passing Stone Mill. A road from the town end of Mill St. went northwards on the line of what was later to become the Cheadle Turnpike (Old Rd.) With the possible exception of Mill St. or Mill Lane it is unlikely that our present street names were in use at this time.

Within the triangle formed by these roads were all the needs of a religious establishment.[11] The stream, known as the Cottars' Brook[12] (now Scotch Brook) flowed through the land, with a mill on the site of Stubbs' Mill and another at *Stone Mill*, this latter referred to at the dissolution as "two water mills under one roof". Between the mills was the fish-pond, where the canons caught, or kept, the fish for the Friday meals; this pond has been filled in as a result of extensions to industrial premises in Mill St. Along the King's highway would be such buildings as the almonry and the guest house, as well as the gate-house; here, and along Mill St. would also be barns and stables, and the buildings where wool and other produce from the *Priory Farms*, were stored, convenient for inspection by purchasers.

The great *Priory Church* consisted of nave, south aisle and transepts, with perhaps a tower over the crossing, and stood about half-way between the present church and the part of Lichfield St. made in 1770. The south transept probably opened up a flight of steps into the dormitory, over the sacristy and chapter-house; the monastic buildings ran from the church towards the King's highway, and the south side of the cloister would be occupied by the dining-hall and kitchens.

Some of these monastic quarters were built over a cellarage or vaulted undercroft[13] which still remains in part. The chapter-house was near to the spot in the present Priory garden where the base of a wall and the lower part of a Norman arch (which remained well into the 19th century) are still visible. A *chapel* on the north side of the church, perhaps the north transept itself, was destined to be of importance, after the dissolution, as the chancel of a second parish church.

The *Prior*, as head of this establishment, was in a position of considerable importance. Not only was he the representative of the church over a wide area; he was also the business head of the priory, and the dispenser of alms to a variety of people travelling along the rough trodden earth roads of that time.

From quite an early date Stone was semi-independent of the mother-house at Kenilworth. Though the parish church of Stone was evidently a wealthy one, the decisive factor in the growth of the priory was its adoption by the Stafford family as "their" monastery. As a result it was not destined to remain one of the small houses of Austin canons which were characteristic of the order in England. In the long-run, daughter houses of regular canons did obtain their independence, and Stone managed this in the late 13th century. A decree of the Bishop of Lichfield and Coventry in 1260[14] allowed that

> "Henceforth the *Prior of Stone* might receive Canons to that habit and profession and freely dispose of everything both spiritual and temporal, appertaining to them, without the allowance of the Prior of Kenilworth, and that the said Prior of Stone, and every one of the Canons there serving God, with their successors, should be free and exempt from any future subjection to the Prior and Convent of Kenilworth for ever ... And that all such charts of Kenilworth as might be of use to the canons of Stone should be transcribed, and transcripts attested with the seals of the said Bishop and prior of Kenilworth, and upon necessary occasion the originals to be delivered to the Prior of Stone or his certain attorney, for the defence of that house and prosecution of their rights."

This arrangement was confirmed by Bishop Roger in 1279[15] and in 1291 a final agreement was made[16] by which Stone retained all the lands and churches which had been granted to it, and undertook to pay yearly to Kenilworth 12½ marks sterling. This agreement was confirmed by King Edward III on August 16th 1339.

From the fragments of the Priory now remaining, it is not easy to picture the size and magnificence of such an establishment. A visit to Haughmond Abbey, in Shropshire, is helpful in this connection. The remains there are extensive; it, too, was a house of Augustinian canons; and like Stone, Haughmond was built on a sloping site, so that a general, if not detailed, comparison is possible.

NOTES AND REFERENCES

1. S.H.C. II. Pt. 1.
2. S.H.C. VI. Pt. 1, p. 2.
3. St. Mary's, Castle Church.
4. See Plate 1.
5. July 24th.
6. Close Rolls, Henry III., 1247–1251, p. 476.
7. S.H.C. VI. Pt. 1, p. 242.
8. Close Rolls, Edward II., 1313–1318, p. 311.
9. S.H.C. VI. Pt. 1., p. 25.
10. Nov. 21 to Feb. 2.
11. See Plate 4.
12. The stream was originally linked, in name, with the "Cot-land". Cot-land was the land allotted for ploughing, and a "cottar" was a lower type of villein, sometimes called a bordar; he had probably a cottage and garden, or small holding of about 5 acres. The land would probably be allotted by the Priory to such of the townspeople as were employed by them, either on their farms, or otherwise in connection with their establishments.

The adding of an initial 's' to words of this type is not unusual, and from "Scottars' Brook" the present form is an easy corruption. Within memory a row of cottages at the side of this stream, off High St., was known as Scotland Yard. The name has no connection with the 1745 invasion of Bonnie Prince Charlie's Scottish troops, who never reached Stone.

13. See Plate No. 6 for this and other remains of the Priory.
14. Chetwynd's History of Pirehill Hundred (S.H.C. XII (N.S.) pp. 102–6., and C. H. Ribton-Turner: Kenilworth Castle (Courier Series of Guides, Leamington) pp. 47–48.
15. Register of Bishop Godfrey Giffard, 1268–1301 (Episcopal Registers, Diocese of Worcester, vol. II., p. 105, fol. 85 (lxxxiiij)).
16. Chetwynd: History of Pirehill Hundred.

CHAPTER 5

STONE PRIORY: DECLINE AND DISSOLUTION

The importance of Stone Priory is made clear by an assessment in 1235–6 of 2 marks, the same as the Priory of Trentham. No other Augustinian house in Staffordshire approached this figure. In 1288–91, for a tax to support the Scottish Wars of King Edward I., *Stone* was rated at 60 marks per annum, the same as Stoke-on-Trent, and one of the largest in Staffordshire.[1] Moreover, in 1312, the priory was granted a general licence to acquire lands and rents to the annual value of £20, "on account of the devotion which the King bears to St. Wulfad, whose body rests in the church of the priory of Stone."[2]

In 1310, for Edward II's Scottish expedition, a large number of the religious establishments were called upon to supply victuals for the army. Of eleven monasteries in Staffordshire, only three supplied more oxen, and only one more wheat than Stone. Stone's contribution of oats (100 quarters) and sheep (60) was not exceeded by any other house.

The Priory had its troubles, too. These were in part due to the disturbed state of England beginning in the reign of King Henry III, with the Civil War between king and barons. For people away from the main stream of events, as those in Stone would be, the result was disorder and lawlessness which affected local life until the close of the 15th century.

Early in 1263, forces under William la Zouche, Justiciar of Chester, and David, brother of Llewelyn, Prince of Wales, had captured Stafford and Chartley Castle. As they returned, they burnt the town of Stone, plundered the Priory and destroyed its muniments (title-deeds &c.).[3]

The Prior of Stone himself was not averse to taking advantage of the state of the country. In 1265 "the Abbot of Hulton charged the *Prior of Stone* with having robbed him of 300 sheep, and with having cut down his corn."[4] This case emphasises, too, the value of wool as a produce of the religious houses. In 1339 wool belonging to Stone Priory, worth 22½ marks, was claimed by agents of the Crown, to the exclusion of other would-be purchasers, in return for a promise of payment the following year.

In 1266 the Cellarer of Stone was charged with breaking into the house of a man who was still a prisoner in the hands of the barons.[5]

Civil war, followed by Scottish wars, brought heavy and repeated taxation. In 1327, "for the defence of the Kingdom against the Scots", 24 Stone residents paid a total of 36 shillings[6] and a further subsidy in 1332–3 realised 38s. 4d.[7] In 1340, at the beginning of the Hundred Years' War, Parliament levied the Inquisition of "the Ninth", based on the assessment of 1288–91. The valuation then had been 60 marks; the jurors found that in 1341 the "ninth" was worth no more than 22½ marks.

Even the courts had been affected by the unrest. In 1294 the *Prior* had maintained his right to 60 acres of land in Walton,[8] and had clashed with the

Peulesdon family who had, through marriage, succeeded to the Walton properties of Ernald. A concord was made by which the family acknowledged certain lands to belong to the Prior, and for this settlement one of the canons was to perform daily service at the altar of the Holy Cross in the *Priory Church* for the souls of members of the family.[9] It is in connection with these law-suits that we learn of a mill at Walton in 1293, and "open fields" there in 1295. From these open fields Joan de Peulesdon claimed a right of way direct to her manor of Walton, but this was successfully challenged by the Prior.[10]

In 1293 the same family claimed before an Assize at Stafford that the Prior and three others had unjustly dispossessed them of eight acres of *heath* in *Walton*. The Prior said they had no common right of pasture in the heath, but only a right of way for their cattle. The jury found in favour of the Peulesdons, but the prior afterwards gave 20 shillings for a jury of 24 to convict the last jury of a false verdict.[11]

Throughout all this disturbed period, the Stafford family had remained loyal patrons of the Priory. Millicent of Stafford's son *Hervey*, who died in 1237, and his wife Pernell, had been buried in the sacristy. Her grandson, *Robert de Stafford IV* was buried with his two wives by the altar of St. John the Baptist. Robert IV's son, *Nicholas de Stafford II* was, in 1287, buried before the high altar.

Edmund de Stafford was buried in the Friars Minors at Stafford, and his son, *Ralph*, was, in 1372, buried at Tunbridge. Ralph, Lord Stafford, was a great warrior. He was present in 1340 at the Battle of Sluys, between the English and French navies; he conducted the defence of Aiguillon against the host of France, fought at Crécy in 1346 and was at the siege of Calais when the six burghers surrendered the keys. He was chosen as a Knight of the Garter when that order was founded in 1348. He was created Earl of Stafford in 1351, and died in 1372.

Hugh de Stafford, 2nd Earl, also served in the French wars, and was made a K.G. in 1375, but became more interested in politics when he married a daughter of the Earl of Warwick. He died in 1386, on a pilgrimage, at Rhodes; he and his wife Philippa were buried at Stone. "in a fayre tomb before the high altar".

Ralph's son, *Thomas*, 3rd Earl, died at Westminster, in 1392, but was buried at Stone Priory, on the north side of the choir near his parents. Thomas's brother, *Sir Hugh*, was also buried in the choir, "in a fayre new tomb."

The fortunes of Stone Priory were declining badly in the 15th century, and no further members of the Stafford family appear to have been buried there after 1392. Indeed, the quality of some of the priors and canons was deteriorating long before then. In 1348, for instance, *John, the Prior of Stone*, and *brother Stephen* de Ashbourne, a monk of Stone, entered the close of Roger de Pulton at *Hilderstone*, stealing goods and chattels to the value of £20.[12]

Lawlessness in the Stone district reached a climax around 1414, when *Hugh Erdeswyke* of *Sandon* was the leader of a faction responsible for many outrages. He appears first in 1413 for contravening the statute of 1390 against maintenance and liveries, designed to suppress the keeping and arming of bands of hired retainers. On the Thursday before Christmas Day, 1413, Hugh Erdeswyke, armiger, had delivered three yards of cloth of livery to John Smith of Stone, yeoman, Robert and Ralph Orchard of Milwich, yeomen, Robert Locwode and Richard Glover of Stone, yeomen.[13] Following this, Hugh and his brother Robert Erdeswyke, Ralph Vykers of Milwich, Ralph Say of Stone, Richard Glover of Stone, had collected from "divers parts of England, Ireland and Wales, disturbers of the peace" to the number of 1000 men. This private army had assembled on the Sunday before the Feast of St. Matthew (Sept. 21) at Amerton, near Chartley, armed for war with "coats of mail, palets, breganders, breastplates, lances, certelhaxes, bows and arrows." Their plan was to kill Edmund de Ferrers, the lord of Chartley, and to pull down and destroy the manor house and park of Chartley. They had maintained themselves for two days by force.[14]

In 1414 the Sheriff was ordered to produce upwards of 300 of these "rebels" to answer for "divers transgressions, extortions and contempts." None of them appeared. Eventually a number of them obtained pardons, and it is a shock to find among them *Ralph de Stamford, the prior of Stone*, an accessory to the death of Ralph Page, killed by Roger, brother of Hugh Erdeswyke.[15]

No sooner had the Hundred Years' War ended in 1453 than the Wars of the Roses began, bringing a further period of social disorder, during which *Stone* suffered both from its own residents and from wandering bands of wrong-doers.

John Johnson, corveser,[16] was a notorious character of this period. On August 3rd 1477, he broke into the close of *Robert Wyse, the prior of St. Wulfad's, Stone*, cut down and carried away 4 pear trees, 6 apple trees, 20 small ash trees, 20 small oak trees, and 200 cartloads of underwood, to the value of £10.[17] No result of this case is recorded, but only four years later Johnson was associated with the Prior, and with Thomas Geslyng of Stone, tailor, John Yelyns and Richard Badnall of Stone, yeomen, in taking by force, on December 19th 1481, the horse of Richard Middlemore, armiger, at Stone. The horse was worth 5 marks; they were further charged with "insulting, beating and wounding his servant Richard Weralle and detaining him prisoner there for ten days, so that he lost his services for a month", for which he also claimed £20 as damages.[18]

There is no evidence of Johnson ever being brought to court, any more than was John Bylstone, late of Doxey, who was charged in 1484 by Robert the Prior of Stone "for breaking into his close and houses at Stone in the time of his predecessor, Thomas, late prior of Stone, and taking 190 sheep worth £20."[19]

The Thomas mentioned here was Thomas Wyse, elected prior in 1439. He encountered serious difficulties over priests for the church, and over internal discipline. In 1446 he had been allowed by the Pope to "staff" the church of Stone (which, it must be remembered, was for the people of the district as well as for members of the order) with one or two canons because "for the most part secular priests are hard to find, and it is not distant from the said monastery."[20]

There was also serious domestic dissension, and the community was split by

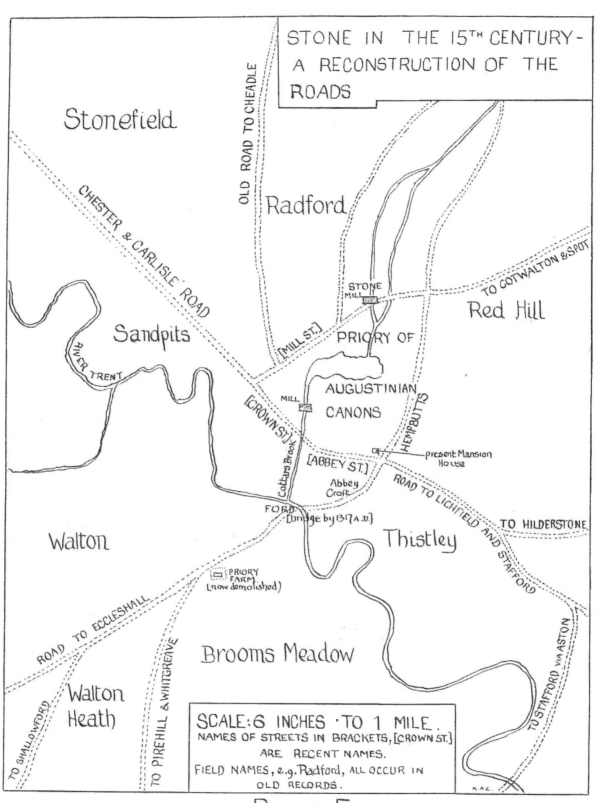

STONE IN THE 15TH CENTURY - A RECONSTRUCTION OF THE ROADS

Stonefield

OLD ROAD TO CHEADLE

Radford

CHESTER & CARLISLE ROAD

Sandpits

RIVER TRENT

STONE MILL

TO COTWALTON & SPOT

Red Hill

[MILL ST.]

PRIORY OF

AUGUSTINIAN CANONS

MILL

[CROWN ST.]

HEMPBUTTS

present Mansion House

Cottars Brook

[ABBEY ST.]

Abbey Croft

ROAD TO LICHFIELD AND STAFFORD

TO HILDERSTONE

FORD
[bridge by 1317 A.D.]

Walton

Thistley

ROAD TO ECCLESHALL

PRIORY FARM
(now demolished)

Brooms Meadow

TO STAFFORD VIA ASTON

TO SHALLOWFORD

TO PIREHILL & WHITGREAVE

Walton Heath

SCALE: 6 INCHES · TO 1 MILE.
NAMES OF STREETS IN BRACKETS, [CROWN ST.]
ARE RECENT NAMES.
FIELD NAMES, e.g. Radford, ALL OCCUR IN
OLD RECORDS.

PLATE 5

unjust words, malice and wickedness. The Auditor of Causes drew up a number of rules for the government of the priory, and Wyse was asked to swear to observe them. He did not do so, and was excommunicated by the Auditor. The Prior appealed to the Pope, and in the summer of 1450 the sentence of excommunication was conditionally lifted. Then, on the initiative of the patron of the house (Humphrey de Stafford, 6th Earl of Stafford, created Duke of Buckingham in 1444), to whom the strife within the "family" priory must have been a source of grief, four Abbots visited *Stone Priory* in December 1450 to find a remedy for the ills that beset the house. They found that the communal life of the house had largely broken down, a not uncommon feature of late mediaeval monastic life. Choir and cloister were neglected; the canons mixed too freely with secular persons; the refectory was no longer used for meals, and drinking and gossiping after compline were usual.

Discipline had to be tightened, with more regular attendance at services. Each canon was to receive an annual salary of £1.13s.4d., for his clothing and necessities. Plots in the priory garden were to be assigned each year, and cultivated for the common good of the priory, and not for private gain. Similarly the profits from the bees kept in the garden and in the cemetery were to be assigned to the sacrist's revenues.

The officers of the priory were to be appointed on the advice of the community, and were all, including the prior, to render annual accounts. The common seal was to be kept under three locks, the keys being held by the prior, the sub-prior and sacrist. The canons' shaving and the laundering of their clothes were to be paid out of the common revenues, and the canons were strictly forbidden to employ private laundresses.

The injunctions laid down as a result of this visitation were ratified early in 1451 by the Duke of Buckingham as patron, by Bishop Booth and by Archbishop Stafford. But the orderly life these new rules envisaged was not easy to attain in those turbulent days, and in 1458 the Suffragan Bishop was commissioned to bless and reconcile the priory church which had been polluted with bloodshed.

A visitation of 1518 shows that there were only six canons and two novices, and the canons were unwilling for their numbers to be increased. Even so, by 1521 there were eight canons, though the two novices complained that only the sacrist could teach them Latin. During these same years there was trouble with the sub-prior, who objected to the presence in the priory of a man named *Onyons*, a glover, and his family. The sub-prior was then described as "a drunkard and much given to hunting."

The new ideas of the Renaissance had already, in the early Tudor period, brought many and varied criticisms of the church, and in particular of the monasteries. As the story of *Stone Priory* has shown, irregularities had been apparent for many years to official visitors; the type of canon and novice had fallen badly in quality; and often the management of monastic properties was inefficient.

Cardinal Wolsey had suppressed several very small religious houses to finance his college at Oxford, and King Henry VIII later suppressed twenty more for his own benefit. There was, therefore, little difficulty in getting Parliament's approval for the closing of those monasteries whose yearly value was below £200. On examination, the financial position of *Stone Priory* was this:[21]

	Receipts	Expenditure	Balance
Temporal	£ 54 12s. 11d.	£ 3 13s. 5d.	£ 50 19s. 6d.
Spiritual	£ 84 9s. 11d.	£15 14s. 6d.	£ 68 15s. 5d.
Totals	£139 2s. 10d.	£19 7s. 11d.	£119 14s. 11d.

Stone was, therefore, well below the income level decided upon, and was included in a list of condemned religious houses published in 1536.[22]

The Commissioners were to visit each religious house to examine accounts and compile inventories; the Prior was to receive a pension; the canons were either to accept posts as priests, or transfer to other houses. Even so, the procedure was not so clear to the individual houses concerned, where there was widespread ignorance and uncertainty.

William Smyth, Prior of Stone, was making extensive repairs or alterations to his priory; for this purpose he had purchased timber out of Blore Park[23] from Bishop Roland Lee. He wrote urgently: "touching the timber which I bought and paid for to my Lord: 40 trees are still standing, as the bearer can show. If I have not the said timber, I know not where to be provided for my great work now in hand."[24] Bishop Lee, far more worldly-wise, and more knowledgeable of the way things were going, had prevented the trees from being felled and delivered to the dying priory.

There were also attempts by interested parties to influence the fate of the religious houses. *Henry, Lord Stafford*, wrote to Thomas Cromwell, telling him "that the *Prior of Stone* hathe good hope that his house schall stand, whereof all the contree is right glad, and praye fulle hertily for your lordship therefore." Lord Stafford was influenced, of course, by the fact that many of his ancestors lay buried in the priory. It was all a vain hope. Along with Trentham and Ranton, Stone was among the first Staffordshire houses to go, and an order was issued to surrender all charters, and the seal, and all plate and other effects.

A documentary fragment[25] shows how the *Canons* tried to prevent the agents of the dissolution taking away all their treasures:

"Articles and instructions for the King's commissioners . . . concerning the embezzling and taking away of certain plate, jewels, ornaments, goods and chattels of the late monastery of *Stone*, whereupon as well William Smyth, late prior of the said house, James Collyer, James Atkyn, Sampson Greswike, Geoffrey Walkeden and Hugh Rathebone . . . are to be examined . . . Whether *Collyer* received a shrine, four standing cups, and two salts of silver; whether *Atkyn* received certain sheep and cattle" since the date when everything became the property of the King.

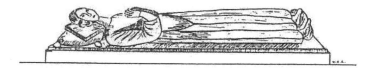

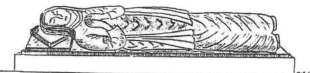

Effigies of an Austin Canon (above)
and a lady, formerly in the Priory Church,
now in the west porch of the Parish
Church. Based on old prints in the
William Salt Library, Stafford.

REMAINS OF STONE PRIORY

Norman Doorway of the Priory, as it was in
the mid-19th. century. Based on a sketch by
J.C.Buckler, 22nd.June 1841 (British Museum)

Remains of the undercroft, or crypt,
of Stone Priory, preserved under the present
Priory. Based on a drawing in 1911
by J.H.Beckett, F.R.I.B.A.

PLATE 6

Certain it is that the Prior had mortgaged a shrine of silver to *James Collyer* for £20, for the Augmentation Accounts of 1538 note that only £13 6s. 8d. of this had been paid.

After the decision to close Stone Priory was final, Lord Stafford took steps to have removed from the condemned building the alabaster monuments to members of his family there. John Leland records that from Stone the images which lay upon these tombs "were caryed to the Freers Augustines in Forebridge, alias Stafford Grene."[26] The times must have been terribly unpredictable for Lord Stafford to carry out such a difficult and costly business as the moving of these images to the Austin Priory at Stafford, when the house was itself to close within a matter of months.

The buildings and site of *Stone Priory*, with the church, steeple and church-yard, and 177 acres of land, were sold to *George Harper, Sir William Pykeryng and George Robynson, mercer, of London*, and the heirs and assigns of Harper for ever. There were 55 acres of arable land in the fields called *Red Hill, Thistley* and *Radford*, and in the common field of Stone called *Stonefield;* also 9 acres of meadow in the fields called *Broad Meadow, Shepley Meadow, Horse Meadow* and *Oak Meadow;* there were 12 acres 3 roods of pasture in the closes or pastures called *Longfurlong, the Orchard* and the *Hempyard;* 101 acres of wood in the woods called the *Walk Mylne Wood, Highwood, Fernehurst Wood* and *Shepley Wood;* two water mills under one roof called *Stone Mills;* a pasture called *Micklows* with an old house therein; and a close of land called *Brooms Meadow*."[27]

Harper soon re-sold the land and the buildings: *James Collier of Darlaston* and *William Crompton* (later described as "*of Stone Park*") then appear to have bought equal shares in the Priory estates, each paying £1,500. Crompton's portion included the Priory buildings, and land roughly to the south and east of the Priory; while Collier held land to the north and west of Stone, towards Darlaston where he resided.

For many years the representatives of the Crown continued to sell properties and land. In 1538, *James Collier*, now described as a draper, purchased a tenement known as the "*Antelope*" with garden, orchard, and a meadow called *Makeley More*, in Stone.[28] In 1540 Sir John Gyfford of Chillington, in Staffordshire, obtained a "*water mill in the parish of Stone*".[29] Robert Darkenhall, in 1541, obtained a "messuage" called *Carrehouse*.[30] *William Plante*, a butcher in Stone, obtained priory land in Walton. The work of disposal was still going on in 1546 when Hugh Rathebon was made bailiff and collector of the Priory lands in Stone.

And so, as *William Smyth, the last prior*, went away with his pension of £20, and the canons departed to start life elsewhere, the great Priory of Stone was left to its fate. Its land sold, its proud monuments removed, its records scattered, the fabric, except those parts for which a secular use was found, was exposed to the despoiler and to the ravages of time and weather. The *Church*, which had formed an integral part of the priory, was allowed to remain as the Parish Church, and was to survive ior two more centuries before the last portion collapsed.

In *1719* the remains of the Priory were described as "ample" when a certain Mr. Arblaster visited Stone. In his notes he wrote:

"There now remains the old Hall. It has a stone Hearth in the middle of it, and a Lanthorn for smoke to ascend at the Top. At the upper end of it is a Place raised with boards, much like unto the upper-end of the Hall at Christ-Church-College in Oxford. Out of this there goes a short pair of stairs into a large room, where, I suppose, the Monks withdrew to converse a little after dinner. On the outside of the Hall is cut, in wooden figures, 1253. There are many little Chambers adjoyning to these, from whence I descended into the Cellars, which were very spatious and large. There are many stone Arches, almost like Church windows. Under one there is part of a vault, which is said to have been half a mile in length, and that it was made for the monks to walk in."[31]

By 1789 the portions remaining were much reduced. "On the road side at the south end of the town, near the site of the Church, is still visible a fragment of the *Abbey*, and I remember, about 14 years ago, when that new road[32] was made, a considerable piece of the wall was demolished for that purpose, and also in the foundation several subterranean passages were discovered by the workmen, though nothing very curious then appeared."[33]

Since the description was written many changes have taken place. The "visible fragment" in the account was almost certainly the beautiful Norman arch which stood in the Priory garden until the mid-19th century. After the present parish church was built in 1753–8, a rectory was built over the remaining vaulted cellars of the old Priory. It was a rector of the day who took down this arch, and used the stone to build a pig-sty. The base of this arch and a portion of adjoining wall remain 'in situ' in the garden of the present Priory, which has now become offices and flats. Strengthened now by steel, the vaulted undercroft, or crypt, still remains in part beneath the present offices. The two stone figures in the west porch of the present church are from the ruins of the old Priory, and, in 1962, during work for a laundrette at the corner of Lichfield St. and Church St., a length of old wall was revealed beneath the shop front. Many shaped stones, with dog-tooth ornament and foliage carving, remain in the Priory garden and in the neighbouring area, and a goodly portion of the walling in Abbey St. is of stone from the monastic buildings. Mediaeval floor tiles and fragments of glass from the Priory have also been found.

Robert Garner wrote in 1844[34] that several rudely formed coffins had been found, presumably of stone, but gave no details. It is known that in 1828 workmen digging foundations near the Parsonage House (present Priory) struck a tiled pavement, and two feet below that a grave nearly six feet long, formed of rough stones. No remains of a corpse were found, except a portion of long auburn hair which, thought the British Museum, could have been Saxon, but could not verify owing to the absence of the other evidence which, as so often, has been lost or re-buried.

PRIORS OF THE AUGUSTINIAN HOUSE AT STONE

Ralph, occurs between 1138 and 1147.

Humphrid, occ. 1155.

Roger, occ. 1161 and between 1174 and 1176.

Robert, occ. 1193 and previously.

Silvester, occ. 1194.

Richard, occ. 1197 and 1203.

Henry, occ. early in Henry III's reign.

Reginald, occ. 1228.

Gilbert, elected Abbot of Haughmond in 1241.

Humphrey, occ. 1246.

Roger of Worcester, occ. between 1266 and 1279.

John Tiney, occ. 1292 and 1294.

Thomas de Mulwich, occ. 1296 and 1305; died by March 1309.

John Attelberge, occ. 1309, died 1327.

John of Stallington, elected 1327, died 1349.

Walter de Podemore, occ. between 1349 and 1362, died 1391.

William Madeley, elected 1391, died 1402.

Ralph de Stamford, elected 1402, resigned 1423.

Thomas Holegrave, elected 1423; elected Prior of Kenilworth in 1439.

Thomas Wyse, elected 1439, occ. as late as 1473.

Robert Wyse, occ. 1477, resigned 1493.

Thomas Fort (Suffragan Bishop) elected 1493, elected Prior of Huntingdon in 1496.

William Duddesbury, elected 1496, died by March 1507.

Richard Dodicote, elected 1507, died 1524.

William Smyth, occ. 1529; prior at the dissolution.

THE SEAL OF THE PRIORY

The seal used by the Priory on its documents in the 13th century has been preserved.[35] It is a pointed oval, 2½ ins. by 1½ ins. and shows the Virgin, crowned and seated, with her Child on her left knee, and holding a flower in her right hand. The legend: "SIGILLUM ECCLESIE SANCTE MARIE ET SANCTI W...... (M)ARTIRIS DE STANIS" is a clear indication of the dedication of the church to the Blessed Virgin Mary and St. Wulfad.

NOTES AND REFERENCES

1. John Ward: History of the Borough of Stoke-on-Trent, p. 454.
2. Cal. Pat. 1307–13, 458.
3. Annales Cestrienses (Lancs. and Chesh. Rec. Soc. xiv).
4. F. A. Hibbert: Monasticism in Staffordshire, p. 85.
5. F. A. Hibbert: op. cit. pp. 118–120.
6. S.H.C. VII. Pt. 1., p. 200.
7. S.H.C. X., Pt. 1., p. 92.
8. S.H.C. VI. Pt. 1., p. 14.
9. ibid. p. 231 (n).
10. ibid. p. 300.
11. F. A. Hibbert: op. cit. p. 44; S.H.C. VI. Pt. 1., p. 101.
12. S.H.C. XII. Pt. 1., p. 87.
13. S.H.C. XVII., p. 6.

14. ibid. p. 7.

15. ibid. p. 26.

16. shoemaker (Halliwell's Dictionary of Archaic & Provincial Words).

17. S.H.C. VI. Pt. 1. (N.S.) p. 130.

18. ibid. p. 134.

19. ibid. p. 135.

20. Cal. Papal Regs. ix., 475–6.

21. F. A. Hibbert: op. cit. pp. 118–120.

22. Letters & Papers, Henry VIII. Vol. X, par. 1234.

23. Part of the Bishop of Lichfield's Eccleshall estates, which included the Offleys and Blore Heath.

24. Letter & Papers, Henry VIII., Vol. X, par. 324.

25. ibid. Vol. XII., Pt. 1., par. 531.

26. John Leland: Itinerary in or about the years 1535–43; vol. V, p. 21.

27. Letters & Papers, Henry VIII., Vol. XIII., Pt. 1., par. 889(2).

28. ibid. Vol. XIII., Pt. 2., par. 734(30).

29. ibid. Vol. XV., par. 942(42).

30. ibid. Vol. XVI., par. g. 1391(47).

31. Note-Book of Mr. Arblaster, 28 April 1720, printed by Oxford Historical Society in "Hearne's Remarks and Collections" (Society's Publications, vol. VII., p. 122).

32. Lichfield St. from the "Mansion house" to High St.

33. The topographer, June 1789: a History and Description of Stone in Staffordshire, pp. 116–124. See also William White: History, Gazeteer & Directory of Staffordshire, 1851.

34. A Natural History of the County of Stafford, London, 1844, p. 116.

35. W. de G. Birch: Catalogue of Seals in the British Museum, i, p. 759; British Museum Seal Cast lxxii, 43.

CHAPTER 6

DEVELOPMENT UNDER THE TUDORS

The whole of the country, towards the end of the 15th century, was longing for respite from strife, waste and insecurity, and the people of Stone were among the earliest to know of an impending change of dynasty in 1485. Henry Tudor, Earl of Richmond, had landed at Milford Haven on August 7th, and marched with 2000 men through Shrewsbury to Stafford. Meanwhile Lord Stanley had moved south to Newcastle and *Stone*, leading his "knights and esquires", banners flying at the head of their companies.[1] Sir William Stanley, coming from the castle of Holt to Northwich, with his men ("all the North Wales and most of the flower of Chester") also moved south to Stone. King Richard III was relying on the support of the Stanleys, but while Henry Tudor was at Stafford, a private message was conveyed by a "certain parson", and Sir William went to talk with Henry in the county town. From Stafford Henry moved, via Wolseley Bridge, into Leicestershire, where, at Bosworth Field, on August 22nd he defeated Richard III and became King Henry VII. During the battle, in which Richard was killed, the Stanleys had switched their support to Henry.

Even after Bosworth, the English army was maintained. In 1508 Stone supplied "*twelve archers and four billmen*" for the "retynue of Sir Thomas Lovell, Knyghte, for the warres"[2] and in 1518 Henry Smyth of Stone, a sherman or clothmaker, went to Calais with Sir Richard Wingfield.[3]

In 1539 Stone supplied *42 archers*,[4] "all abull men with bowes and have hernes (equipment) and artillarie (weapons) as foloith their names:

Thomas Alkyn	Alexander Wagge	John Coton
Hugh Raboon,	John Cradock	John Wildblood
hernes for a man[5]	William Warrelowe,	William Smyth
John Crompton	horse and harnes	John Badnoll,
William Allen,	for a man	a salett
a pair of splentes	Robert Porter,	Thomas Smyth
Ric. Fynnye	horse and hernes	Robert Leech
William Clomer,	for a man	Thomas Mount
a dossen arrows	John Porter,	Harrie Hawkyn
John Helley	horse and hernes	Robert Webbe,
Ralph Bennett	for a man	a peyr of splentes
Ralph Clerk	James Johnson	Roger Mabbon
Robert Dale		John Poton
John ap Jenkyn		William Hunte
John Barnold,	William Coton,	Ralph Bate
a jack and a bill	a bill	Roger Crosse

These persons foloing have hernes and artillarie as foloith their names:

Roger Mason,	Thomas Barnefelde,	Ric. Blakhurst,
a sallett	a gestern[6] and	a sallett
Thomas Reve,	a bill	Homfrey Cartwright,
a sallett		a jack"

These names represent the ordinary families of Stone, who must have welcomed the greater order now prevailing, and the increased efficiency of the law. As an example, Henry VIII had ordered that the *Bible translated into English* be placed in every church. The Court of Star Chamber enforced this, and summoned the parson of Swynnerton "for keeping the Bible out of the church."

In the town of Stone *the market* had been revived under the licence granted to *Robert Colyer* of Darlaston (lord of the manor of Stone) in 1549.[7] The *Stanley* family owned extensive lands in *Aston*, and their family tombs used to be in the Priory Church. The *Unett* family was already established at Tittensor, and the *Beardsmores* were at Beech. A will[8] dated June 22nd 1555, has been preserved; it begins:

"I *Steven Beardsmore of Beech*, in the parish of Stone, sick . . ." He desired to be buried in the parish churchyard of Stone, and he left the residue of his goods to his wife for life, "and keeping my name and unmarried". "All waynes (carts or wagons), plowes, yokes and other stuff belongynge to husbandry with half the mock (muck), and two whiches (chests), with all the alelomes (heirlooms), fattes (vats or casks), tornelles (tubs), bordes, formes and one cupboard" were to remain between his wife and his son John.

Another son, William, was to have "bordes to make him a whiche (chest) of the same value as the better is in the house, and fellyes (outer wooden rim) and spokes to make him a pair of wheels."

At *Stone Park* the *Crompton family* was now well established, the Stone branch having descended from two London citizens, members of the Fishmongers Company and Clothiers. *William Crompton*, who in 1539 had brought Priory lands, was undoubtedly a wealthy man, for in 1562 he purchased Apedale and other Staffordshire land for £1000. He was buried on December 16th 1579; his wife Catherine died on June 25th 1582.

It was clearly understood, when Crompton bought the site and buildings of the priory, that the church would remain as the Parish Church of the district. It was in the care of two curates, both of whom paid a tax of 5s. 4d. in 1533, and in 1540 they paid a subsidy levied on the income of religious persons.[9]

During the reign of Queen Mary, when Roman Catholicism was restored, and its opponents persecuted, *Richard Clyffe*, assistant curate, left Stone (where a number of powerful Catholics lived) to become vicar of Sandon. He returned to Stone after Mary's death, and from 1559 regularly received the salary of £5 6s. 8d.

Churches which had formed part of a monastic establishment found themselves very impoverished in the years after the dissolution. This is the Inventory of Church Goods at Stone at the beginning of October 1552 for Edward VI's Royal Commission:[10]

"First: 2 copes (cloaks or mantles), the one of satin bruges, the other of white tuke.
Item: 2 vestments of yellow satin bruges with amices (oblong white linen worn round the neck under the alb) and fans.

Item: 9 old vestments, one old cope with 2 albs (white linen vestment), one amice and
     stoles (scarves)
Item: 2 surplices, 2 altar cloths, 2 chalices of silver with patens.
Item: 2 crosses of maslen (maslin, a type of brass), a brass censer (for incense) and 3
     bells in the steeple.
Item: One little bell, 4 brass candlesticks, and a bucket of brass."

The impoverishment of the church soon spread to the fabric, too. In the time of Edward VI the *Parishioners of Stone* sent a petition[11] to the Lord Protector Somerset, stating that

"... *their own parish church*, in which all manner of sacraments had, from time out of mind, been ministered to themselves and their ancestors, was formerly united, annexed and joined to the Abbey Church, and that there was also *a chapel* standing thereby, wherein the town of Stone had, for their own ease and convenience, been holding their daily services, except for the administering of the Sacraments and the Rites on certain principal Feasts in the year. *William Crompton had lately attempted to pluck down the said church and had uncovered a large part thereof, and conveyed away the lead to his own private use*, although the King's Commissioners had suffered the church to remain after the dissolution of the Priory." They begged that Crompton be called to London to answer the complaint. It is not known whether Crompton did explain his action; it is known that for the next twenty years the church continued to decay, and the chapel alone remained safe for services.

On May 24th 1558, six months before Elizabeth I succeeded Mary Tudor as Queen of England, an elderly clergyman wrote a codicil to the will he had made a few days earlier. The clergyman was *Thomas Alleyne*, a former Rector of Stevenage, in Hertfordshire.[12] By this codicil he made Trinity College (Cambridge) trustee of the vast estates which he had acquired in the few years before, using funds left to him for charitable purposes in 1547 in the will of his brother Ralph. At his death, the College was to establish *three free Grammar Schools*, at Uttoxeter and *Stone* in Staffordshire, and at Stevenage; to pay each of the schoolmasters £13 6s. 8d. a year; and to draw up rules for each school.

Thomas Alleyne's estates included nearly 700 acres at Tillington, on the northern edge of Stafford[13], the tithes of which went to the Cromptons of Stone. The old clergyman was a friend of the Cromptons, and in a surviving portion of the priory buildings a school had been started[14] even before Thomas's death in August 1558. It would be·here that Trinity College continued the school, a grammar school in the original sense, with the emphasis on Latin and religious knowledge. All conversation in school was to be in Latin, and failure to obey this and other rules was punishable by the rod. Holidays were few, and hours of work long, though normal for the period: mornings from six (seven in winter) until eleven: afternoons from one till five. A few of the boys attending the school were educated free; others paid fees varying from 10s. for a lord's son to 4d. for sons of those dwelling in the town. There were probably about 20 boys studying

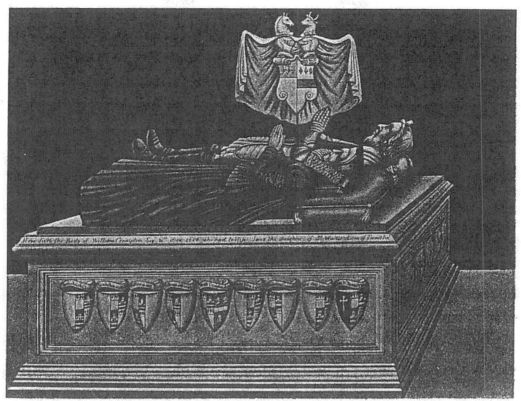

The tomb of William Crompton, who died in 1603 (not 1606 as shown on this print) and of his wife Jane. Formerly in the chancel of the Priory Church, this tomb is now in Stone Parish Churchyard.

The Thomas Crompton brass, now in Stone Parish Church.

Both illustrations are from old prints in the William Salt Library, Stafford, and are reproduced by kind permission of the Trustees of the Library.

PLATE 7

in a single room of the old priory, while all around materials of every kind were removed, and the priory buildings became more ruinous.

By 1572 the small chapel on the north side of the decaying church was the only portion of the building fit for use, and all services were being held there. It was considered beyond the resources of the parishioners to repair what they then called the "Abbey Church", owing to the greatness of the structure and the decayed and fallen down state of it. Supported by Thomas, Bishop of Coventry and Lichfield, the parishioners sought leave to take down all but the chapel, and use the materials for building an aisle, or nave, on to the chapel, so making a serviceable parish church for the town and district. Matthew Parker, Archbishop of Canterbury, granted a licence[15] for the work on June 10th 1572, and ordered that "the said chapel and new aisle built on to it shall be constituted as the parish church according to the custom and form of the other churches of this realm." Barnabas Willatt, in 1602, received £10 13s. 4d. in salary as curate of this 'rebuilt' church.

The position of this chapel can be judged by the position of the Crompton table-tomb in the parish churchyard. In 1663 Ashmole described this tomb as being on the south side of the chancel (i.e. the chapel) There it remained until 1749 when the collapse of this second parish church damaged it, and left it exposed to the elements.

After the strong swing back to Roman Catholicism in the reign of Mary Tudor, Elizabeth I had tried to follow a line of Protestant moderation. But at *Aston* there was a strong element of the old religion which objected to Elizabeth's order of compulsory attendance at church. In his list in 1577 of "all such persons, gentlemen and others, within the countye of Stafford which come not to Churche to heare Divine Service", Bishop Bentham named "Dorothy *Heveningham*, widow; Thomas Whistons, schoolmaster to her son; Thomas Lawnder, her servant; John Bradbury, her chaplain; and Anne, wife of Robert Collier, esquire."

The Bishop estimated Dorothy Heveningham's income from her land at £40 yearly, and her total income at £433, so that she was a person of considerable importance. In 1581 the Privy Council named her as "one of the most obstinate and dangerous Recusants of Staffordshire". In 1588, the year of the Spanish armada, close watch had to be kept on these Catholic sympathisers. The list for that year included, besides Dorothy Heveningham, the widow, Mary Heveningham, spinster, Elizabeth the wife of Thomas Beardmore yeoman, Katherine Comberforde spinster, John Bobytt yeoman, Richard Turner yeoman, Edmund Porter husbandman, all of the parish of Stone. With the defeat of the Armada, the danger to Elizabeth from religious factions was ended.

For many people in Stone, however, life was gentle and peaceful in this Elizabethan period. In his will[16] made on June 17th 1567, *John Lees of Stone*, a "smythe" left to his son James "the implements of my smithy with my stiddie[17] and all the rest of my tools when he is of age to practise them himself...and ... to my brother Roger my best coat." *Thomas Cotton of Knenhall*, in his will dated

August 2nd 1577,[18] left "to each of Thomas Phillips' children a lamb, and to either of Thomas Blore's children a lamb."

The *Parish Church Registers* tell us that in 1570 wheat was 17s. a quarter, eggs were 2s. a dozen, pigeons were 10d., a fat goose 1s. 2d., a fat sheep 3s., and an ox £2. A stonemason was paid 6s. and a common labourer 5s. a week. A pair of shoes could not be bought for less than 12d., and when a blacksmith shod a horse the charge was 10d. or 1s.

In the Tudor period, *alehouses* had to be registered. In 1536 John Brasnell, shoemaker, received a licence, sureties being given by Thomas Cotton of Stone, salter, and by William Webb, shoemaker. The constables of Stone in 1594 were George Asberie and John Baylie; they listed 53 victuallers and badgers (these were itinerant licensed dealers in food-stuffs); there were no chapmen (hawkers) nor pedlars.

The reign of Elizabeth I also marked the establishment of *Stone as a post-Office* in the original sense, an office with a master of the Posts who was to "keepe three horses at least contynuallie in the stable bothe Winter and Somer, or have them so neere unto his house that the furthest he maie be ready to depart with the pacquette within one quarter of an houre after he heareth the boye or man blowe his horne that bryngeth it." On the post road from London to Holyhead, Stone was the only Staffordshire town mentioned in 1573 in a *list of postmasters* preserved at the Public Records Office:

"*The Poste of Stone—William Nicholson* for his wagies servinge her Majestie by the space of CLI days at xxviii miles at xx d. per diem . . . £12 11s. 8d."

The time taken for a letter to travel from Chester to St. Albans in 1598 was 31 hours, for the times were noted on the back of a letter: left Chester at 6 in the evening of Sunday, the 11th of July 1598; Nantwich at 10 that night; Stone at 2 on Monday morning; Lichfield at 8; Coventry at 11; Daventry between 3 and 4 in the afternoon; Towcester between 5 and 6; Brickhill at 8 that night; and St. Albans at 1 o'clock on Tuesday morning.

Towards the end of this Elizabethan age, there was living at the old *Darlaston Hall*, a poet whose work has associated him with Shakespeare. He was *Richard Barnfield*, born at Norbury in 1574. In 1594, two years after graduating at Oxford, Barnfield published his first volume, "The Affectionate Shepherd", and in the following year a second volume "Cynthia, with certain sonnets and the Legend of Cassandra". The third and last book appeared in 1598, and in this appeared two poems which were included in the "Passionate Pilgrim" in 1599, under the mistaken impression that they were Shakespeare's work.

The sonnet begins
        "If music and sweet poetry agree . . ."

and the ode
        "As it fell upon a day
        In the merry month of May . . ."

After the publication of this third volume, Barnfield seems to have settled down as a country gentleman at Darlaston. There he died, his will of February 27th 1627, showing him to have been in affluent circumstances. He was buried in the parish church of *St. Wulfad at Stone* on March 6th 1627 at the age of 53.

It is only of late that something like justice has been done to the great poetical qualities of Barnfield, to his melody, and his picturesqueness. That he knew Shakespeare personally is almost certain, and it is no small honour, as the Dictionary of National Biography says, to have written poems which everyone until our own day, has been content to suppose were Shakespeare's.

NOTES AND REFERENCES

1. Nicholls: Leicestershire, IV., p. 552, quoted by John Ward: History of the Borough of Stoke-on-Trent, p. 411.
2. Army Lists of May 1508.
3. Letters & Papers, Henry VIII., Vol. II. Pt. 2., par. 4200.
4. Muster Roll of 1539 (S.H.C. V (N.S.) p. 283).
5. harnes for a foot soldier: a jack (padded leather jacket), a salet (light, steel helmet), pair of splints (armour for the arms) and a gorget (to protect the neck).
6. a sleeveless jacket, on which were fastened small, overlapping plates of steel.
7. See plate 1.
8. Stafford Wills, 13 (S.H.C. 1926, pp. 9–10).
9. Letters & Papers, Henry VIII. Vol. XVI., App. 1.
10. Hutchinson: Archdeaconry of Stoke-on-Trent, p. 187.
11. S.H.C. 1915, p. 259.
12. For a detailed study see Norman A. Cope: Alleyne's Grammar School, Stone, 1558–1958. See plate 13.
13. Land sold by Trinity College in 1957; now a housing estate known as Trinity Fields.
14. "To him which taught the school at Stone next before Snr. Cooke (first appointment by the College) . . . £5." (Trinity College, Bursar's Book, 1559–60).
15. Canterbury and York Society Publications: Canterbury Diocese, part XCIII., pp. 1036–1038. Register of Matthew Parker, part 9, folio 69.
16. Stafford Wills, 66 (S.H.C. 1926, pp. 48–49).
17. stithy or forge.
18. Stafford Wills, 67 (S.H.C. 1926, p. 49).

CHAPTER 7

STONE IN THE SEVENTEENTH CENTURY

"A great parish and market town"[1] was the description of Stone in 1604. During the first thirty years of the 17th century we learn of the people in Stone mostly through land transactions[2]: Challenor and Rathebone, the Cromptons, Vernons, Astons and Bowyers.

Robert Challenor was one of our earliest *postmasters*, as well as being *innkeeper* and landowner, and he held the post for nearly forty years, succeeding Hugh Rathebone who occurs in 1599. In 1635 a royal proclamation set up a service of messengers for conveying letters along eight main roads, and it was made illegal for letters to be carried by private messengers. In a petition of 1637 Challenor claimed that during a serious illness, an attempt had been made, with the aid of a £40 bribe, to get him out of his position on the grounds that he was unfit. He had, in fact, never failed in his duty, being assisted in his illness by his son, and he produced certificates to this effect from the Justices of the Peace. The petition made it clear that the Stone postal stage was the longest one between London and Chester, and that arrears of pay due to Challenor amounted to £368. *Thomas Challenor*, the son, succeeded his father as postmaster shortly before the outbreak of the Civil War in 1642.

This Chester road through Stone was "one of the six prime post ways, and readiest for Ireland, and one of the most frequented roads of the kingdom."[3] Along this road *in 1620* came *John Taylor*,[4] known as the "Water Poet", who "travelled on foot from London to Edinburgh." After receiving much hospitality, he had a rough passage between Lichfield and Newcastle:

"At night I came to a stony town called Stone,
Where I knew none, nor was I known of none:
I therefore through the streets held on my pace,
Some two miles further to some resting-place."

His resting-place was in a field, under an improvised shelter of branches, in an all-night downpour.

In *1638 Richard Braithwaite*, author of "Drunken Barnaby's Four Journeys to the North of England", also visited Stone. He was suspected of being a Jesuit, and was searched, but his bundle of papers turned out to be playing-cards:

"Thence to *the Bell* at *Stone* straight drew I.
Delia, no Diana saw I.
By the parson I was cited,
Who held me for Jesuited;
In his search, the door fast locked,
Nought but cards were in my pocket."[5]

It is generally agreed that the *Bell* visited by Braithwaite was the *Blue Bell*, which formerly occupied the site of the Town Hall. It was on land which had formerly belonged to the priory; it had become possible to develop this land for building after the dissolution. A road was developed from the present Market Square to the lower part of the town, known for a long time as Market St., and on either side of this road inns such as the Crown, Blue Bell and Bell and Bear were able to provide extensive stabling and, later, coach-yards.

The *curate* at *Stone Church* was now *Barnabas Willatt*, who first occurred in 1597 and who was buried at Stone in April 1640. He received a salary of £10 13s. 4d. in 1602, and £11 in 1604, when the parsonage of Stone was valued at £200. Willatt had no degree, and was described as "no preacher". Fulford chapel was still connected with Stone, and the curate there was "commonly a boy". Barnabas made this entry in the church registers on January 20th 1632:

"I, Barnabe Willatt, curate of the Parish of Stone, within the county of Stafford, knowing that mistress Jane Hocknell, of Darlaston, hath long been sick, and yet is weak in body and very sickly, do hereby licence the said Jane Hocknell, during the continuance of her sickness and weakness, to eat flesh on fish days, according to that power and authority given me." A number of other people also received this licence.

An assistant curate of this period was *John Lightfoot* (1627–29). He was a keen Hebrew scholar, and coming from his studies in London to say farewell to his parents in Stoke before going abroad, Lightfoot was persuaded to serve the church in Stone. In 1628 he married Joyce, daughter of William Crompton of Stone Park, but he soon found that in Stone he was too isolated from the libraries necessary for his studies, and left his curacy the following year.[6]

This *William Crompton of Stone Park* was the eldest son of the William Crompton who had bought the Priory lands (and who had died in 1579). The second William died in 1603, and his wife Jane, daughter of Sir Walter Aston of Tixall, died in 1626. Their tomb was originally on the south side of the chancel of the church which had been rebuilt in 1572, but is now in the churchyard. The figures on the tomb are in Stuart dress: Jane has the large ruff, long dress entirely covering the feet, and square-toed shoes; William wears the light armour of the period, and his neck rests on a helmet; the lower parts of his legs were broken off when the church collapsed in 1749.

At the eastern end of the tomb is the Crompton coat-of-arms, and on the north and west sides are 14 shields, one for each of the children of the marriage. William Crompton was Sheriff of the County of Stafford in 1597, and a Justice of the Peace in 1597 and in 1602.[7]

His younger brother is commemorated by a brass,[8] 22 ins. by 18 ins., showing the kneeling figures of *Thomas Crompton*, his wife Etheldred Tusser, and their 4 sons and 2 daughters. Here Thomas wears typical armour of the period, with tassets or thigh pieces made very large to enclose the trunk hose, and with riveted shoulder plates. The inscription begins: "Here lyeth Thomas Crompton,

Esquire, one of the Honourable Band of Pentioners to the high and mighty Prince James, King of Great Britaine . . . &c." but it fails to record that he died in 1619.[9] This brass was also in the chancel of the old church; it has been restored, and is now in the south aisle of the Parish Church (S. Michael).

The centre shield on the north side of the Crompton table-tomb represents the 5th child, *Thomas*, born about 1580. He became a Justice of the Peace in 1608, and in 1614 he was elected Member of Parliament for Stafford County. Thus *Thomas Crompton*, son of a merchant, was the first representative for the county for nearly 200 years to come from outside the old county families. Indeed, of 31 members elected for the county between 1603 and 1715 only ten were untitled, and two of these were Cromptons.

Although he favoured the Puritans, Thomas Crompton refused to raise forces in Staffordshire without the King's authority, when Parliament ordered him to do this in September 1642. He maintained his attitude, even when his eldest surviving son became a prominent member of the Parliamentary committee at Stafford. In fact, in May of 1645, *King Charles I* stayed for two nights as an uninvited guest at Stone Park, prior to the Battle of Naseby. The diary of one of the King's officers, Captain Symonds, recorded:

"Thursday, May 22.
We marched from Drayton to Stone in the county of Stafford. His majestie lay at Mr. Crompton's house, a sweet place in a fine park. He a rebel.
Friday: the army rested.
Satterday 24: We marched to Uttoxeter."[10]

Less than two months later, Crompton had died (July 8th 1645).

Staffordshire remained clear of the major conflicts of the Civil War, and was rather the scene of sporadic and gentlemanly conflicts between garrisons and leaguers, and between small companies (of each side) which seemed to wander about the countryside. One of the fiercest of these clashes was at Hopton Heath in 1643, when Sir John Gell's Parliamentary troops, having drained quart pots at the "Dog and Doublet" at Sandon, and plunged their heads into the vats in the cellars, were narrowly defeated by a Royalist troop coming out from Stafford.

Later, in 1643, with Lichfield surrendered and Eccleshall Castle captured, the Parliamentarians were able to establish themselves in the county town, and exercise control over much of the county.[11] The Stone district then experienced most of the inconveniences of war: the collection of weekly money payments; the quartering of troops; the requisitioning of carts, horses, timber, oats and hay; and restrictions on the movement of individuals. Many families around Stone lost their lands (until the Restoration) by the order of 1643 which gave Parliament power to seize the personal property, lands and revenues of those who opposed Parliament, and two-thirds of the possessions of those who were papists. This order affected the Sneyd and Leveson families, the *Heveninghams of Aston*, *the Colliers of Darlaston* and the *Fitzherberts of Swynnerton*, whose house was ordered to be demolished to prevent its use as a garrison, and the *Heamies Farm* in Chebsey parish was taken from Peter Giffard. Stafford was the garrison town with the responsibility for gunpowder, and an unique form of exploitation was that undertaken by the saltpetre-men, whose unattractive commodity was an indispensable raw material for gunpowder. There was a deal of digging for saltpetre as far afield as Stone: on September 11th 1644 it was ordered that "what liquors for Saltpeeter shall be got by the workmen in or neare to the Towne of Stone shall be boyled in Mr. Challenor's furnace there for the saveinge of the carriage."[12] This was, of course, *Thomas Challenor, innkeeper, and postmaster* after 1642. In 1643 he had been held prisoner at Stafford "for goinge into the Enemies garrison without licence." After entering into a surety of £100 to the speaker of the House of Commons not to do "any thing that shall be preiuditiall to the King and Parliament", it was ordered that "Mr. Challenor shall be forthwith enlarged" (set free).[13]

The Stafford Committee was not without sympathy to residents when the need arose. A certain Capt. Robert Grosvenor had the greatest part of his estate captured by the Royalists, and he was forced to rely on his friends for accommodation and for the care of his children. In particular he was helped by "Richard Bryan of Walton by Stone", and it was, therefore, ordered that Richard Bryan should, in the circumstances, be exempt from having troops quartered on him.[14]

The curate at Stone Church after 1642 was *Deliverance Fennyhouse, M.A.*, and with this typically Puritan name it was natural that he supported the county administration, and that he was rewarded accordingly:

"10 April 1644. That Mr. Fynnyehouse, mynister of Stone, shall have for the augmentation of his mainteynance (because his contributions are smaler in these hard tymes) and for his paines in helping to gather the rest of the tithes, shall have the Easter Rolls of Stone, and the tithes of piggs and geese for the yeare to come; above the yearlye paye of twenty marks, which hath been ancientlye belongynge to the Mynister there."[15]

The Civil War brought the first outstanding headmaster to *Stone's Grammar School* in the person of *Thomas Chaloner, M.A.* An enthusiastic teacher and friend of learning, Chaloner had become head of Shrewsbury School,[16] and by the outbreak of the war was already building up a good reputation for his teaching. When Charles I visited Shrewsbury in September 1642, Chaloner, a royalist, made him a loan of £600 from the well-filled school chest, but four years later, when Shrewsbury had fallen under Puritan domination, his position was untenable, and he was forced to leave. From then until 1662, when he returned to Shrewsbury, he wandered from place to place, trying to follow peacefully his work as a schoolmaster or tutor, but always harassed by the many Parliamentary prohibitions, and once even by the plague. In the course of these wanderings he came to *Stone* in *February 1649* to find the school without a master. On the first day he entered 37 names in his register, and at the end of the month there were sixty names. It is hard to know what caused him to leave Stone. It may have been Parliamentary pressure, although Thomas Crompton, a strong Parliamentarian, paid 10s. on the first day for his young son William to be taught by Chaloner. Perhaps it was the death of his wife, who was buried in Stone churchyard. By June 1650 he had moved on, leaving a bright episode in the early history of the school.

Puritanism was now in the ascendant, but still finding it necessary to deal with its opponents. The estate of *Francis Colier* of Stone (and Darlaston) had been sequestered during hostilities, but the Coliers' resistance went on even after the execution of the King, and on May 23rd 1649 a warrant was issued "to apprehend Francis and Walter Colier of Stone for uttering treasonable words and endeavouring to raise a new war."

During the period of the Commonwealth, *Thomas Crompton* of Stone was typical of the new order. He was baptised on June 25th 1607, and is often remembered because he had four wives and served on no less than seven commissions. But he was also a Colonel in the Parliamentary army, and very active in the county. Early in 1650 he was proposing to raise 400 horse in Staffordshire, and he did soon afterwards raise 200 horse and 100 dragoons for the Scottish expedition which ended with the victory of Dunbar. While Cromwell was still in Scotland after this victory, Prince Charles (later Charles II) crossed the border and headed south in support of his father's cause. The Parliamentary forces gave chase, but on August 19th 1651 they had only reached Manchester. Prince Charles had, on this very day, quartered his army in Stone before pressing on to Lichfield. By taking an easterly route, Cromwell cut off the Royalist forces and defeated them at Worcester on September 3rd. After his escape from the battle, Prince Charles was back in Staffordshire, at Boscobel House, where he hid in the famous oak tree. This was virtually the end of resistance to the Commonwealth, and two Stone soliders, Thomas Clarke and John Preston, were discharged from military service in November 1652.[17]

Thomas Crompton sat as Member of Parliament for the county from 1647 to 1653, and again in 1654–5, 1656–8 and 1659–60. His house at Stone Park was the first "home" of the *Nonconformist religion in Stone*. John Machin of Seabridge, near Newcastle-under-Lyme, set aside £8 12s. a year for the provision of a *double lecture* to be given by the principal ministers of the county on the last Friday in every month at the following towns in rotation: Newcastle, Leek, Uttoxeter, Lichfield, Tamworth, Walsall, Wolverhampton, Penkridge, Stafford, Eccleshall, *Stone* and Mucklestone. The lecturers were to receive 13s. 4d. each for their services, and 12 honest poor men who heard the lectures were to be given one penny each. The lecture was given first at Newcastle on August 4th 1650, and the series went on until the beginning of 1660, when the changed circumstances made its continuance impossible.[18] The first lecture at Stone would have been in about May 1651, and it was at the home of Thomas Crompton that the meetings took place.

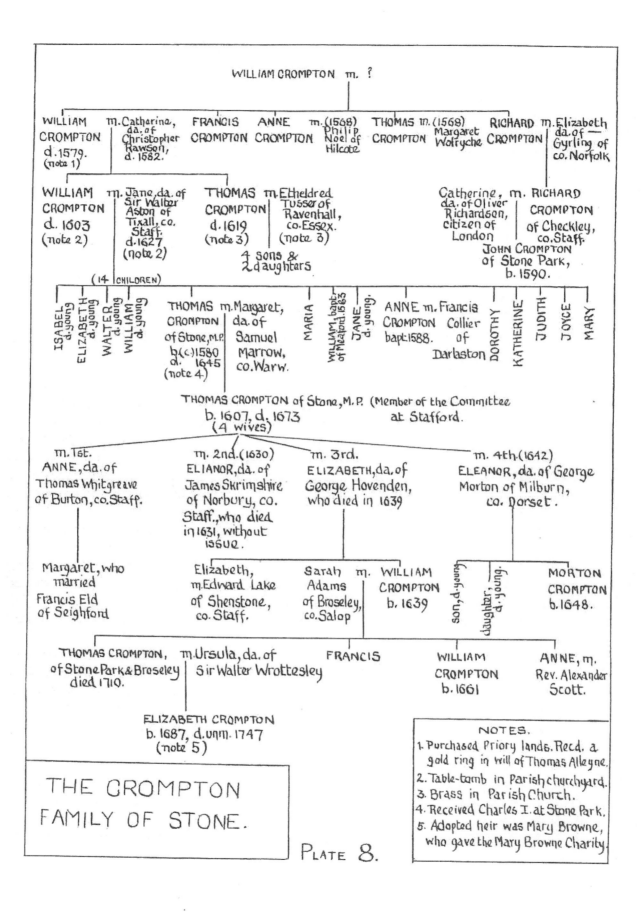

WILLIAM CROMPTON m. ?

WILLIAM CROMPTON d. 1579. (note 1) m. Catherine, da. of Christopher Rawson, d. 1582.

FRANCIS CROMPTON

ANNE CROMPTON m.(1568) Philip Noel of Hilcote

THOMAS m.(1568) CROMPTON Margaret Wolryche

RICHARD CROMPTON m. Elizabeth da. of ─ Gyrling of co. Norfolk

WILLIAM CROMPTON d. 1603 (note 2) m. Jane, da. of Sir Walter Aston of Tixall, co. Staff. d. 1627 (note 2)

THOMAS CROMPTON d. 1619 (note 3) m. Etheldred Tusser of Ravenhall, co. Essex. (note 3)

4 sons & 2 daughters

Catherine, m. RICHARD da. of Oliver Richardson, citizen of London

CROMPTON of Checkley, co. Staff. JOHN CROMPTON of Stone Park, b. 1590.

(14 CHILDREN)

ISABEL d. young

ELIZABETH d. young

WALTER d. young

WILLIAM d. young

THOMAS CROMPTON of Stone, M.P. b.(c.)1580 d. 1645 (note 4) m. Margaret, da. of Samuel Marrow, co. Warw.

MARIA

WILLIAM, bapt. of Meaford. 1583

JANE d. young.

ANNE m. Francis CROMPTON Collier bapt. 1588. of Darlaston

DOROTHY

KATHERINE

JUDITH

JOYCE

MARY

THOMAS CROMPTON of Stone, M.P. (Member of the Committee at Stafford.
b. 1607, d. 1673
(4 wives)

m. 1st. ANNE, da. of Thomas Whitgreave of Burton, co. Staff.

m. 2nd. (1630) ELIANOR, da. of James Skrimshire of Norbury, co. Staff., who died in 1631, without issue.

m. 3rd. ELIZABETH, da. of George Hovenden, who died in 1639

m. 4th. (1642) ELEANOR, da. of George Morton of Milburn, co. Dorset.

Margaret, who married Francis Eld of Seighford

Elizabeth, m. Edward Lake of Shenstone, co. Staff.

Sarah Adams of Broseley, co. Salop m. WILLIAM CROMPTON b. 1639

son, d. young

daughter, d. young

MORTON CROMPTON b. 1648.

THOMAS CROMPTON, of Stone Park & Broseley died 1710. m. Ursula, da. of Sir Walter Wrottesley

FRANCIS

WILLIAM CROMPTON b. 1661

ANNE, m. Rev. Alexander Scott.

ELIZABETH CROMPTON b. 1687, d. unm. 1747 (note 5)

THE CROMPTON FAMILY OF STONE.

NOTES.
1. Purchased Priory lands. Recd. a gold ring in will of Thomas Alleyne.
2. Table-tomb in Parish churchyard.
3. Brass in Parish Church.
4. Received Charles I. at Stone Park.
5. Adopted heir was Mary Browne, who gave the Mary Browne Charity.

PLATE 8.

The Restoration of the monarchy came quietly to Stone, and to many the first significant change would be the placing in the parish church of a painting of the Royal coat-of-arms, which now hangs in the south gallery. Although the Crompton family continued as the most important family in Stone, politically its influence was at an end. Indeed, there was a reaction against non-conformity which at one time seemed to endanger Thomas Crompton. This was in 1664, when "Colonel Thomas Crompton of Stone" was named as "implicated in treasonable designs". His name appeared on a list of suspects in 1665, reported by the Lord Lieutenant of Staffordshire as "intended to be secured", but it was never done.[19]

Thomas lived on until 1673, in the pleasant surroundings of Stone Park, where, according to a survey of parks in 1660 by Sir Simon Degge, there were deer. When he died, *Eleanor*, his widow, had his remains laid in the Crompton table-tomb (then inside the Priory church); a brass plate on the south side of the tomb, previously blank, records this. There are now no remains of the monument which Eleanor erected to his memory in 1676.

The Stone estates then passed to William, the son of the third marriage (with Elizabeth Hovenden), who was born in 1639. He became a J.P., and in 1683 or 1684 he purchased the *manor of Stone* from James Colier for £600.

The son of this William Crompton, another Thomas, married Ursula, the eldest daughter of Sir Walter Wrottesley. He acquired from his mother, an Adams, extensive properties at Broseley in Shropshire. This last Thomas died in 1710, and the only child of his marriage with Ursula was a daughter *Elizabeth*. She died unmarried on April 13th 1747, at the age of 60, her monument in Broseley Church describing her as "the last heir of that ancient family."[20] Her sole executrix and adopted heir was Mary Browne, whose name is recorded on the Benefactions Boards over the north stairs of Stone Parish Church:

"*Miss Mary Browne, of Broseley*, by deed dated Nov. 28th 1755, gave a charge of 35 Pounds per ann. on Stone Park, also certain tithes, and a piece of land called the Pools, the income to be paid to the Officiating Minister of Stone Parish Church." By this charity the Crompton family is for ever linked with the town and the parish church.

The Benefaction Boards in the Parish church record many charitable bequests for the poor of the district, and they emphasise the gap which must have been left by the dissolution of the monasteries, who had always cared for the needy. The first poor law of Queen Elizabeth I in 1563 enacted that "two able persons or more shall be appointed gatherers and collectors of the charitable alms of all the residue of the people inhabiting in the parish"[21], and these collectors were to distribute weekly the parish alms to poor and sick people, and to keep records.[22] Money to pay for this came from the charitable bequests, from fines for the breaking of certain laws, and from the poor rate which the overseers were empowered to levy.

Two old record books of the *Stone Overseers* have been preserved,[23] the first one commencing: "The Accounts of *Gabriell Barnes, Overseer of the Poor of Stone* for the year *1691*." In those days people in receipt of parish relief wore a badge with a large P, along with the first letter of the parish,

> "1700. pd. for Bages for ye poor to put upon their shoulders   ..   ..   ..   £00 01 00"

Sometimes assistance took the form of goods:

> "1698. pd. Mary Baker to buye her a (spinning) wheel ..   ..   £00 05 00"

And the loan of a cow was very helpful in time of sickness:

> "1728. pd. Wm. Barlow in his illness £02 01 00
>   pd. for a loan of a Cow for him   ..   ..   13 02"

Medical attention was simple, and often given by the more capable townsfolk:

> "1703. pd. for letting John Moat blood 9 times in his sickness £00 03 00
> "1730. paid Francis Watson for setting Widow Tildesley's Leg 11 00
> "1735. Nov. 30. pd. James Robinson for Drawing (Widow Elkin) a Tooth
>   and Bleeding 1 00

Swearing was an offence of which the law took cognisance, and the Parish Church has a copy of an Act of Parliament imposing these *penalties for swearing*:
"For every day labourer, common soldier, common sailor, common seaman —one shilling.
For every other person under degree of gentleman—two shillings.
Every person of or above the degree of gentleman—five shillings.
Second conviction, double, and third, treble, these fines."[24]
At this time Marlborough was fighting on the continent, and in need of troops and the *press gang* was at work even in Stone; the parish often had to care for the dependants:

> "1706. pd. two women their Husbands being impressed £00 03 00
> 1707. pd. John Cookes Wife £00 02 08
>   pd. her since her Husband was impressed 00 10 03½

Money was also required for the war; a grant was made by Parliament to His Majesty "of certain Rates and Duties upon Marriages, Births and Burials, and upon Bachelors and Widowers for the term of five years, for carrying on the war with France with vigour":

> "1697. pd. for the King's Duty for the burial of 2 paupers £00 08 00
> 1698. pd. for the King's tax for a man who dyed at the Carr-house £00 04 00

The Overseers dealt with the welfare of orphans, with their 'schooling', with foster homes if they were "foundling children", and in the arranging of apprenticeships. Local traders were obliged to accept a quota of apprentices each year, or pay a sum of money in lieu of each child not taken (£4 in 1738).

Clothing was made rather than bought:

> "1698. 4 yds. of cloath at 8d. per yd. & 4 yds. of cloath for shirts at 10d. per
>
> yd., thrid 2d. £00 06 02
>
> 4 yds. Linen cloath, thrid & making for two shirts for Slynn £00 04 00
>
> 1 pr. Stockings, 1s. 4d., tape 1d. £00 01 05
>
> 2½ doz. buttons 3d., thrid 6d., canvas 1½d., stay tapes 1d. £00 00 11½
>
> flannell for pettycoats   ..   ..   £00 03 00"

Thrift was also apparent in these accounts:

> "1737 fore Blew wool to foot theire Stockings at the Workhouse   ..   ..   £00 00 09"

The parish kept in repair certain houses occupied by the poor:

> "1703. pd. for repairing Old Titley's chimney £00 03 06
>
> 1708. pd. for thatching Widd. Harvey's house..   ..   ..   £00 02 00"

The workhouse itself was, at this time, a thatched building, which cost 8s. 4d. to re-thatch in 1743. It was also insured for £1 2s. 6d. per annum against fire, and there was an expenditure in 1735, of 4d. for "putting up" the metal badge which denoted the company to which the insurance premiums were paid. The Overseers ceased to pay fire insurance after 1748 for reasons not stated.

Life in the town still centred around the Priory Church and the streets near it. The parson was "passing rich on forty pounds a year", and lived in a cottage behind the premises of Mr. G. Massey in Lichfield St., probably near the present St. Michael's Hall. There were still open fields to the north and north-west, and through them a narrow country track led to Meaford, leaving the town by North St.[25], and past the Old Hall[26] where the Barbour family lived.

John Emery was a maltster in the town and his son was a tailor. When John was overseer for Stone, his accounts recorded: "To my son for clothing for poor as per bill, £6 12s. 3d." The overseer for Beech gave his order to a Mrs. Plant, a draper in Stone. *Thomas Dawson* was a currier and leather dealer; one of the leading *cordwainers*[27] was *Richard Willatt*, and there was another named *Hewitt*. The local blacksmith was *John Hyatt*, whose smithy was on the spot now occupied by the main Church St. entrance to the Parish churchyard.

The non-conformity which had centred round Stone Park had been suppressed after the Restoration of 1660, and toleration did not come until 1689, when there was a revival of this form of worship, and a meeting-house by 1704.[28] Services were held at the house of *Thomas Haynes*, a tanner by trade, at Pryors Hall in Walton.[29] When this house became too small for the numbers of Independents (or Congregationalists) and Presbyterians who held joint services, a meeting-place was built on some land belonging to John Bradbury, behind the house of Sampson Shelley in High St.[30]

The year 1715 saw the riots against the Nonconformists which coincided with the attempt of the Old Pretender to regain the throne. Meeting-houses at Newcastle, Wolverhampton, Stafford, Lichfield, Uttoxeter, Stone, Walsall and West Bromwich were all attacked, the *damage at Stone* amounting to £135 7s. 6d.[31] After this Thomas Haynes again applied for a licence and joint services were conducted in a building in Crown St., Haynes succeeding King as minister in 1723, and remaining until 1728, when he moved to Nantwich.[32] Stone maintained its Presbyterian meeting-house until 1748; in that year the Stone and Stafford houses united under one minister, an indication of a decline which ended in the Stone one being closed in 1808, and the other some years later.

NOTES AND REFERENCES

1. Puritan Survey of the Church in Staffordshire in 1604 (English Historical Revue, vol. 26 (1911), pp. 38f., and S.H.C. 1915, pp. 258–262). The word 'great' refers to area.
2. S.H.C. XVIII. Pt. 1., S.H.C. VII. (N.S.), S.H.C. VI. Pt. 1 (N.S.)
3. John Ogilby: Britannia, p. 41.
4. Thomas Burke: Travel in England, pp. 30–31.
5. Edition of 1716 (Brit. Mus. 1077, b.18).
6. D. M. Welton: John Lightfoot, the English Hebraist, pp. 12–13; and John Ward: History of the Borough of Stoke-on-Trent, pp. 483–4.
7. For further details of the Cromptons, see the article by T. Pape in the N.S. Field Club Trans. vol. LVII (1922–23) pp. 58–66. See plate 7 for a picture of this tomb when it was inside the church.
8. See plate 7.
9. The parish registers record his burial on June 4th 1619. See also Charles Masefield: The Monumental Brasses of Staffordshire (N.S. Field Club Trans., vol. XLVII (1912–13) pp. 170–171.
10. Stebbing Shaw: History and Antiquities of Staffordshire, vol. I, introd. p. 72. Diary of Richard Symonds (Camden Series, 74, pp. 175–6).
11. See "The Committee at Stafford, 1643–1645", the order book of the Staffordshire County Committee, edited by D. H. Pennington & I. A. Roots, published in 1957 by Manchester University Press in association with the Staffordshire Record Society.
12. ibid. p. 177.
13. ibid. pp. 221–2.
14. ibid. p. 243.
15. ibid. p. 92.
16. See G. W. Fisher: Annals of Shrewsbury School, 1889; and Norman A. Cope: Alleyne's Grammar School, Stone, 1558–1958.
17. State Papers Domestic, 1652–3, p. 248.
18. A. G. Matthews: The Congregational Churches of Staffordshire, 1924, pp. 30–31.
19. ibid. pp. 60–61.
20. S.H.C.V. pt. 2, p. 332. See plate 8 for Crompton pedigree.
21. 5 Elizabeth I., cap. iii, sec. ii.
22. Eleanor Trotter: Seventeenth Century Life in the Country Parish, (C.U.P. 1919) p. 52.
23. County Record Office. A short account appeared in W. Wells Bladen: Stone in Bygone Days (N.S. Field Club Trans. vol. XXIII.(1889–90)) pp. 89–96.
24. N.S. Field Club Trans. vol. XLV (1910–11) p. 210.

25. Now part of Station Rd.
26. Now Stone Rural District Council Offices.
27. Boot and shoe maker.
28. A. G. Matthews: op. cit. pp. 30–31.
29. ibid. p. 126. Later known as Priory Farm (moated) and now demolished for Tilling Drive housing and shop development.
30. A. G. Matthews: op. cit. p. 126.
31. ibid. p. 128.
32. ibid. p. 129.

CHAPTER 8

ROADS AND BRIDGES

During the Civil War and through the Restoration period, the Postal service in the area continued to develop, aided in no small degree by the enthusiasm of *Thomas Challenor*. In 1655 the Commissioners for Staffordshire wrote to the Comptroller of the Posts, petitioning that Challenor continue as postmaster "as hee hath lived in that capacity for many years last past, during which time he hath carefully and diligently conducted himself in time of warr as peace."

Three years later this advertisement appeared in "Mercurius Politicus"; the wording seemed to suggest that Challenor was one of the best-known post-masters on the Chester road:

"All gentlemen, merchants and others who have occasion to travel between London and West Chester, Manchester, Warrington or any other town upon that road, for the accommodation of trade, dispatch of business and ease of purse, upon every Monday, Wednesday and Friday morning between 6 and 10 o'clock at the house of Mr. Charteris, at the Sign of the Hart's Horn in West Smithfield, and postmaster there, and at the postmaster at Chester, and at the postmaster of Warrington, may have a good and able horse or mare furnished at 3d. a mile without the charge of a guide; and so likewise at *the house of Thomas Challenor of Stone in Staffordshire*, upon every Tuesday, Thursday and Saturday mornings to go to London; and so likewise at all the several postmasters upon the road, who will have such set days, so many horses with furniture in readiness to furnish the riders without any stay, to carry them to and from any of the places aforesaid in four days as well to London as from thence, to places nearer in less time."

Challenor took his postal work so seriously that in 1663 he complained of Edward Rathbone and his son-in-law William Pool "who daily horse persons riding post, contrary to the act and proclamation", and again that Edward Rathbone's son John, who was postmaster at Lichfield, had "sent the post-bag by private persons."

In spite of his obvious keen-ness, he was succeeded about 1672 by *Robert Barbour*, who, the following year, had to complain that he was constantly being molested by Challenor. The official reply assured him: "Whilst you continue to do your duty as you ought, you need not fear being replaced by him or anyone else." The position at Stone was so important that Challenor's reluctance to be replaced was understandable. In the "Booke of the Postage"[1] the salaries of the postmasters in the reign of Charles II are recorded:

Postmaster of Stafford . . . . £2. 12s. 0d. p.a.
Postmaster of Lichfield . . . . £30. 0s. 0d. p.a.
Barbour, Stone . . . . £64. 0s. 0d. p.a.

The latter half of the 17th century saw much greater use of the roads, and a change from trains of pack-horses carrying goods to wheeled traffic of all types. The first reference to a stagecoach on the Chester-road had been in 1646,[2] and according to Stow[3] road-waggons were travelling on the main thoroughfares as early as 1654. Towards the end of the century Thomas and John Baddeley were carriers between Newcastle-under-Lyme, Stone, Lichfield, Stafford, Coventry and London.

The introduction of regular services of heavy wheeled vehicles had a deplorable effect on the soft earth roads. Act after act tried to restrict these vehicles, until it was eventually accepted that roads had to be properly maintained, and that the old "statute labour" was no longer adequate.

An act of 1654 provided for a road rate of 1s. in the £, so that the cost of road works could be equally shared, but this Commonwealth legislation was rarely enforced, and became invalid in 1660. The deterioration in the roads was shown by the fact that on April 9th 1657 a coach was advertised in "Mercurius Politicus" to run from *London* to West Chester in four days, to *Stone* in three days for Thirty Shillings, running on three days a week; within the space of two years the time from London to Chester had increased to five days.[4]

The repair of *bridges* was a more complicated business. The law enforced the maintenance of bridges on the persons by whom they had been erected. Obviously this was not easy, and the repair became an obligation upon the parish, or upon two parishes if the bridge was situated between them. The majority of Staffordshire bridges in the 17th century were parish bridges: among them *Sandon* bridge, *Aston* bridge, *Walton* bridge, *Darlaston* bridge and *Strongford* bridge, all over the river Trent.

Darlaston bridge was repaired jointly by the inhabitants of Stone and Darlaston; *Strongford bridge* by the people of Trentham, Stone, Barlaston, Tittensor, Kibblestone, Darlaston and Swynnerton. In some cases bequests were made for the upkeep of bridges. In *1317 Roger Marshall* left 100s to repair the bridge at Walton,[5] and in *1473 Stephen Hawkyns' will* left 6d. to the same bridge. Sometimes it devolved upon the whole Hundred to keep a bridge in repair, as the Pirehill Hundred for Weston bridge[6] and Wolseley Bridge. Where no responsibility for bridge maintenance could be established, it had been laid down by the Statute of Bridges (1531) that the maintenance should fall on the county.

In *1655 Strongford bridge* was carried away by a flood. When replaced, it was still only a horse-bridge, for in the Quarter Session Records for 1709 it was ordered that "Tittensor bridge or Strongford Bridge, standing in London Road, *be converted to a stone cart bridge*, the present bridge though built of stone is only for horses, horsemen and footmen, and in tymes of flood carts and carriages cannot pass and repass, and it is an absolute necessity that it be altered."[7]

In 1660 the County gave £20 for the repair of *Walton bridge*, which had probably suffered also in the floods, for it was stated that "if it is not repaired, it will be totally ruined."[8]

In the year 1662 there was "information pending against the County of Stafford, in the Court of Exchequer, for not repayring *Darlaston bridge*." The Court at Quarter Sessions immediately decided to spend £80 on its repair. The justices appointed to report on the state of the bridge suggested that it be con-

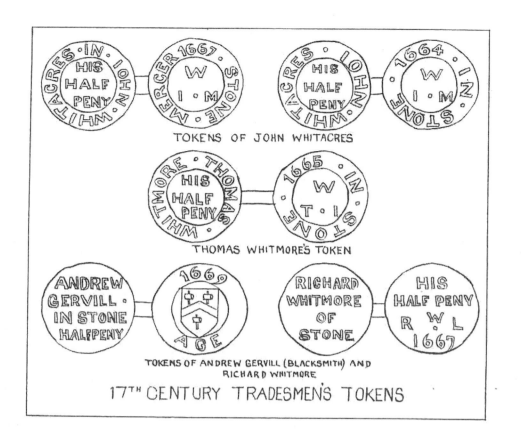

TOKENS OF JOHN WHITACRES

THOMAS WHITMORE'S TOKEN

TOKENS OF ANDREW GERVILL (BLACKSMITH) AND
RICHARD WHITMORE

17ᵀᴴ CENTURY TRADESMEN'S TOKENS

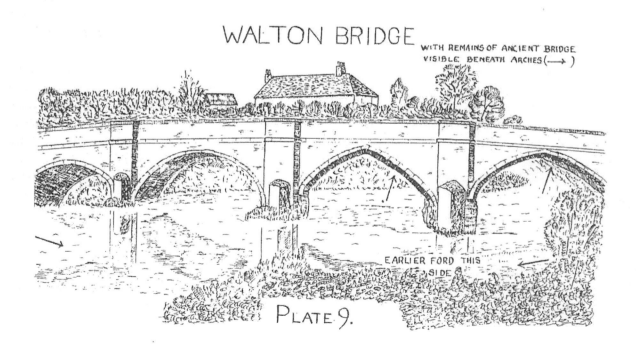

WALTON BRIDGE

WITH REMAINS OF ANCIENT BRIDGE
VISIBLE BENEATH ARCHES (⟶)

EARLIER FORD THIS
SIDE

PLATE 9.

verted into a bridge "for carts and wagons to pass over, the said bridge standing upon a very great road leading from the City of London to the Kingdom of Ireland, itt being now butt a horse bridge, whereby the King's subjects have been, and are, much endangered by reason of floods."[9] The court finally decided that £200 be levied for the conversion of the bridge.[10]

In the town of Stone itself there were about 170 families in 1666. About 70 householders were charged under Hearth-tax or chimney-tax;[11] and some of the houses must have been of considerable size: Thomas Crompton paid on 12 hearths, Thomas Vaughan on 15, Francis Colier on 8, Thomas Chadwicke on 12, Edmund Rathbone on 8, and Ralph Smith on 9. About 100 of the householders were listed as "not to bee chargeable according to the Act."

The number of houses and the chief-landowner in the villages surrounding Stone were recorded in Gregory King's Note-Book, written during a visit in 1680.[12] Walton had 10 or 12 houses (Thomas Leacroft); Aston 15 or 16 houses; Burston 20 houses (Sampson Walkadine); Little Stoke 6 or 7 houses; Carr-house, an inn; Cotwalton 4 houses; Spot 3 or 4; Hilderstone 100 houses (Philip son of Richard Gerard); Fulford 30 or 40 houses (Thomas Foden); Moddershall 7 or 8; Woodhouses 2; Oulton 12 houses (Mr. Val Short); Meaford 8 or 10 houses (Edward Short and William Jervis); Tittensor 20 or more houses (George Unitt of the Hill Top in Tittensor); Beech 20 houses (Ralph Brereton); Darlaston 30 houses (James Colier, son of Robert); Stone Park, William Crompton.

Many of these names recur in 1682 when the Duke of Monmouth made a "royal progress" through England and "touched for the King's evil." Illegitimate son of Charles II. he was at the time being favoured as Protestant successor to the throne in preference to the Catholic Duke of York (later James II). He was met on his way from Lichfield by Mr. Leveson Gower of Trentham and many of the Stone gentry, who entertained him at the "Crown" before he continued to Trentham.

Tradesmen's tokens have preserved for us the names of some of the *Stone trades-people* of the late 17th century. These tokens were issued by traders themselves, because no small coins were then being minted. A *John Whitacres* half-penny[13] was found by workmen laying a gas-main in Crown St. in 1933. Four other Stone tokens have been found, and one found in 1935 on the Coppice housing site had been issued by Samuel Leech, a woollen draper in Warrington.

For a town like Stone, on a main highway, the condition of the roads for trade and travel was of the utmost importance. Roads were now so bad that travellers by coach were said to be weary the first day and almost dead the second. Every other method having failed, the authorities decided to improve the roads by a system of tolls, and the first "turnpike road" in Staffordshire was the 8 mile stretch from Tittensor to Talke in 1714.

In 1728 a *Petition* of the Gentlemen, Freeholders, Tradesmen and other Inhabitants of the *ancient Market-town of Stone"* was presented in the House of Commons.[14] It stated that

". . . the town chiefly depends upon the *Post Road* from London to Chester; and great Carriages to Manchester, Liverpool and other trading towns, passing that way, the same also the route between Lichfield and Stone, are become dangerous to Passengers, and almost unpassable, and the Inhabitants are unable to repair the same; And therefore praying that Leave may be given to bring in a Bill to empower Trustees to erect a *Turnpike* or Turnpikes, and appoint Persons to collect Toll, where most convenient, for the speedy Amendment of the said Roads, and for keeping the same in Repair."

Called to give evidence, *Mr. Robert Barbour*, a former postmaster of Stone, said that in many places

". . . the road is worn deep with heavy Carriages; and although large Sums of Money have been laid out by Contribution, for the Repairing of the said Road, and the Statute-work constantly done, yet that has not been sufficient to put and keep the same in Repair . . . in several places between Cannall's Gate and Stone, and at Darlaston, there are several hollow ways, which render such parts of the Road impassable when any Quantity of Snow falls, and for that Reason many Coaches, usually travelling that way, have left the Road, and Post-boys with Packets have not been able to pass."[15]

Soon there were tolls on the two main highways through the centre of Staffordshire, London to Chester and London to Carlisle, with the exception of a short length from *Darlaston Bridge* to Tittensor, which was not turnpiked until 1799.[16] These developments made for an increase in travellers and in the facilities for their comfort. Whereas in 1673 Stone was "very poor and hath a mean Market on Tuefdays", in 1720 it was a "well accommodated Town with several convenient Inns", and by 1764 it was "well provided with good inns."

Robert Barbour who had given the evidence about road conditions, was postmaster of Stone from 1673 to 1699, when he was succeeded by *Mrs. Jane Barbor*. In 1721 a *Mr. T. Barbor* became postmaster, and soon incurred the displeasure of the authorities. Ralph Allen had, in 1720, been checking on the practice of sending letters without accounting for them in the returns to the Revenue authorities. In one of his letters to the Surveyor of the Midland district he wrote: "Mr. Barbor of Stone, I have always understood, never concerns himself with bye letters,[17] but leaves this business to his uncle", and later: "I will not say that it is impossible that no letter should, during this time, pass between such trading places, but during (your) stay in Stone, I must in a particular manner desire you will examine whether you receive none." Allen had noticed that, according to vouchers sent in, not a single letter in a whole quarter had passed between Stone and Coventry.[18] There was no post-office as yet for the Potteries' towns, and the Longton (Lane End) letters were sent by horse-post from Stone. The final outcome of these investigations has not been recorded.

In 1745 Stone suddenly found itself in the forefront of the national story. Landing in Scotland in July 1745, Prince Charles Edward (Bonnie Prince Charlie) at the head of 6 or 7 thousand supporters, crossed the border, and was in Carlisle by the middle of November. He then decided to march on London, even at the risk of meeting the superior force then mustering in Staffordshire. A private letter, written at *Stone* on November 18th told of these preparations:

"This afternoon an Officer of Brigadier Bligh's Regiment came here with an order to get horses for 200 men going to Chester; they were at Coventry last night, and are to be at Chester tomorrow. Col. Cornwallis commands them. We are boiling of Beef and getting Beds and other necessary Refreshment ready for the poor Men, who will be here about 12 this night . . . Lord Gower's Regiment marched to Chester yesterday morning; their Clothes and arms are to follow them."[19]

The *Duke of Cumberland* was, meanwhile, coming north to take command of this army. A letter from Lichfield on December 2nd recorded:

". . . the Duke came here last Friday, and this morning His Highness and all the army, except Lord Cobham's regiment of Dragoons and Handyside's regiment of Foot, which came in here about noon, left us. . . . The rebels were at Stockport and Macclesfield in Cheshire, and may be in Staffordshire today if they please.

"Much depends upon their march, for by that it must appear whether they intend to come forward and fight, or to retreat the way they came . . . or slip between the two armies[20] by Buxton and Derby . . . and avoid the army which I think they will never face, for our army is about 13,000 good troops, with a large artillery, which last night lay at Rugeley, and is gone today to *Stone* or Stafford, and the rebels by all accounts not above 7,000. . . . The plan of battle was fixed before they left us this morning, and the soldiers received their cartridges. . . . I believe the whole army encamp near Stone tonight."[21]

Another letter, also written on December 2nd, from Rugeley, said: "The Rebels are to be at *Stone* this night."[22] In actual fact the Prince had moved from Macclesfield towards Leek and Derby, while a detachment of troops under Lord George Murray made a feint through Congleton. This latter ruse succeeded: the cavalry at Newcastle were alerted, and two battalions of infantry pulled back to Stone. Cumberland also felt that an engagement was imminent. The artillery moved north from Rugeley, and Cumberland himself marched out of Stafford at 11 o'clock on the night of December 2nd, with three battalions of guards, in order to join the main army at Stone.[23]

So Cumberland's army assembled at Stone, and encamped "on the spacious rising ground to the north of the town called *Stonefield*, in hourly expectation of an engagement".[24] This great expanse of unenclosed land stretched from our present Margaret St. almost to Meaford, and from the heights of Oulton Cross and Old Rd. westwards to the river Trent. Here the army waited, the artillery drawn up on Motley Pits, now left scarred by the digging and throwing up of earth to mount the cannon as high as possible. In addition to the guards there were eleven battalions of foot and six regiments of horse and dragoons. Many of the soldiers were in tents on Stonefield,[25] others billeted in and around the town with a consequent strain on the town's resources. James Ray, a native of Whitehaven, who had joined the Duke of Cumberland's army at Stafford as a volunteer, recorded that "Quarters were very hard to get, it being but a small Town; and so many Soldiers soon occasioned a Consumption in the Victuals and Drink".[26] Another contemporary account found it all "to the great inconvenience and confusion of the inhabitants." *Swynfen Jervis*, who was a barrister living at Meaford Hall, says that he found the streets crammed with soldiers, and *the Duke lying down on straw* in a small room at *Mr. Hinckley's*.[27] Mr. Jervis himself received

CUMBERLAND HOUSE IN HIGH STREET.

THE CROWN IN THE COACHING AGE: THE OLD BUTTER
MARKET IS ON THE RIGHT, AND ON THE LEFT IS THE HOUSE IN
WHICH PETER DE WINT WAS BORN.

PLATE 10

70 soldiers, besides officers, at Meaford, and a bed had been prepared for the Duke, upon the floor, as was his custom, but he preferred to be in the town. John Jervis accommodated 300 soldiers at *Darlaston*. The loyalty of these two Jervis families was emphasised by the fact that *Swynfen's ten year old son, John*, then a boarder at Burton-on-Trent Grammar School, was one of only two boys in the school who did not wear the Pretender's colours.

By the 4th of December news reached the Duke at Stone of the Pretender's swing through Leek to Derby. The Duke called at Meaford to thank Swynfen Jervis for the preparations he had made, before moving away. On the 5th Prince Charles had reached Derby, the limit of his advance, while the Duke had pulled back to Meriden. Once the Pretender began his retreat the Duke set off in pursuit at the head of his dragoons, with 1000 of his foot soldiers mounted on horses provided by the gentlemen of Staffordshire.[29] The battle which was so nearly fought at Stone, was not fought until April of the next year at Culloden.

Swynfen Jervis was an active magistrate, as well as a barrister, and after helping to intercept spies and messengers, he went with Sir Thomas Parker to Carlisle to try some of the rebels.[30] One of the Pretender's staff was captured at Stafford, but afterwards escaped. Two more were taken at Stone. One of these was Richard Vaughan, a prominent Catholic and strong Jacobite. He was caught by the parish constable of Stone when trying to cross the Trent at Darlaston in a bid to reach Wales. He was taken to the "Crown", but no sooner was he there in the custody of the constable when a "gentleman" arrived who wished to interview the prisoner in an inner room. This was the last seen of the prisoner, who escaped through the back door, and the last seen, presumably, of the "gentleman".[31]

The account books of the *Overseers of the Poor* have a number of references to the '45 Rebellion and its aftermath:

"1745. pd. on account of the artillery man who dyed at
           John Sales   ..   ..   £4. 17. 8.
           pd. for the funeral of the man who dyed at George
    .   Shelley's and attendance of him ..   ..   ..   £0. 14. 06.
   1746. June 18. Clothes for the Soldier's child   ..   ..   2. 11.
           Making Soldier's child's coat ..   ..   1.
   1747. pd. to carry a Soulder's wife to the Regiment   ..   3.

The Rebellion remained a subject of conversation in Stone for many years: even in 1789[32] people were still pointing out the house where the Duke slept and telling how the inhabitants were almost dispossessed of their houses.

NOTES AND REFERENCES

1. William Salt Library, Stafford.
2. Sir William Dugdale: Diary, p. 85 (edition of 1827).
3. Survey of London by J. Stow, vol. II., chap. V.
4. Charles G. Harper: The Holyhead Road.
5. S.H.C. XI. p. 31.
6. Ms. Staffs Order of Sessions, vol. VI. p. 57.
7. S.H.C. 1934, pp. 22–3.
8. ibid. p. 23. See plate 9.
9. Ms. Order of Sessions, vol. VIII. (Staffs).
10. S.H.C. 1934, p. 23.
11. S.H.C. 1921, p. 42 and pp. 96–99.
12. S.H.C. 1919.
13. See plate 9, and note spelling on tokens. See also Llewellyn Jewitt: Traders' Tokens of the County of Stafford (N.S. Field Club Trans. 1884. pp. 93–117; and Boyne: Tokens issued in the 17th century (revised edition of G. C. Williamson) pp. 413–4.
14. House of Commons Journal, 17 February 1728. Vol. xxi, p. 222.
15. ibid. 19 February 1728. Vol. xxi, p. 228. The road was turnpiked in 1728.
16. S.H.C. 1934, p. 44.
17. bye letters: letters passing between two towns on the same route, e.g. Stone to Nantwich, or Newcastle to Lichfield.
18. S.H.C. 1934, p. 119.
19. General Evening Post, no. 1896. Nov. 19–21, 1745 (Salt Ms. 2062, iv. 24).
20. General Wade's army was marching south through Yorkshire.
21. Historical Mss. Commission: Mss. of the Earl of Dartmouth, vol. II. p. 165.
22. General Evening Post, no. 1902, Dec. 3–5, 1745 (Salt Ms. 2062, iv.33).
23. The (London) Gazette extraordinary, Dec. 5th., published by authority, price 2d.
24. Stebbing Shaw: History of Staffordshire, vol. I. p. 86.
25. John Ward: History of the Borough of Stoke-on-Trent, pp. 355–6.
26. James Ray: A Compleat History of the Rebellion, 1757, p. 148.
27. No. 8, High St., purchased by Mr. Hinckley in 1719; now aptly named Cumberland House.
28. Correspondence of Swynfen Jervis, Dec. 1745 to Jan. 1746. (Brit. Mus. Add. Mss. 29913, ff.1–2.).
29. Robert Chambers: History of the Rebellion of 1745–6, p. 198.
30. Correspondence of Swynfen Jervis (Brit. Mus.).
31. S. A. H. Burne: Traditional History (N.S. Field Club Trans. vol. 43 (1908–9)) p. 137.
32. The Topographer, May 1789, pp. 63–68 (Excursion from Newcastle to Stone in Staffordshire).

CHAPTER 9

STONE HEROES

The night of Saturday, December 30th 1749, was one which kept the people of Stone talking for a long time afterwards. In the late afternoon there had been, in the parish churchyard, a funeral, that of Mrs. Elizabeth Unitt of Groundslow Fields. At about a quarter past seven in the evening the *church began to collapse*, and at about a quarter to one on the Sunday morning a pillar and two arches fell.[1] This was the original priory chapel and the aisle built on in 1572, all of very old stone, and probably weakened by the installation of six bells, cast by Abraham Rudhall of Gloucester in 1710.

There is no record of how services were held after this collapse of the building, but there is a story that one of the six bells was hung in a large tree, where it could at least be tolled. There it attracted the attention of a traveller passing through the town by coach, who is said to have remarked:

> "Poor Stone, paltry people,
> Got a church without a steeple!
> The farther I travel, the more wonders I see,
> Here's a church with no steeple, its bell in a tree."[2]

Although the disaster must have caused the Rector, Mr. Hinckes, and his churchwardens considerable anxiety over many months, the first recorded facts about the extent of the damage did not appear until January 1753, when a Petition was presented to the House of Commons, in which it was stated:

"The Church is a very ancient Fabrick; the Parishioners have for many years been at a continued Expense in repairing the same; by reason of one of the main Pillars of the said Church giving way, a great part of it is fallen down, and the other Part, which is standing, is so very ruinous that it is incapable of being repaired, and, in the opinion of several able Workmen (who have surveyed the same) must necessarily be rebuilt."[3]

An Act was passed later in the same year authorising the rebuilding of the church, to be carried out in "a manner that may be least burdensome to the Inhabitants of the said Parish". A large number of Trustees were appointed under the act, who, besides being responsible for the actual work of building, were enpowered to raise money by the levying of a Rate on the parish, not exceeding 2s. in the £.

The plan agreed upon was that "drawn by *Mr. Robinson of Greenwich* in the Gothic taste",[4] varied, at the request of the Trustees, to take galleries "such as shall make it more compleat and commodious".

It was considered necessary to build the church on a new site, "on the near end of the Churchyard adjoining to the Row".[5] To make the site large enough a number of properties had to be bought "in a street in Stone called the Row",[6] as well as part of the land known as the Hempyard or Hempbutts. The main work of building was entrusted to *Charles Trubshaw of Great Haywood*:

"I will undertake to build ye carcase of a church according to Mr. Robinson's design for Nine Hundred and Eighty Pounds having all ye Materials found me. And to find all Materials for Twenty Nine hundred and Thirty Pounds. Charles Trubshaw."

The detailed transactions for the rebuilding show that many local craftsmen contributed to the work. For the support of the galleries, for instance, it was agreed that "Mr. Lymer do order Mr. Hopkins to forge Eight Iron Pillars, three inches square."[7] The oak for all the pews was supplied by John Richardson of Cheadle, Timber Merchant, and the work done by William Lymer, also of Cheadle.[8]

The Act of Parliament had stated that:

". . . as soon as the said New Church shall be rebuilt and finished . . . it shall be lawful for the said Trustees to fix a value on the several *Seats or Pews* to be erected and built in the said Church, and to sell by Writing under their hands and seals in simple all or any of such Pews or Seats; and that the Monies arising by the Sale of such Pews or Seats shall be paid to the said Trustees."

This *system of selling the pews* was to cause controversy in the later history of the Church, and was to affect seriously the seating for poorer people. But at the time of the rebuilding it was the means of raising £1413 towards the costs.

The Church was sufficiently finished to allow for its use and consecration on June 21st 1758.[9] For reasons now quite unknown, and certainly hard to understand, the old dedication to St. Mary and St. Wulfad was abandoned, and the new church was dedicated to St. Michael.

The accounts for the rebuilding, up to July 5th 1759[10] showed a total expenditure of £4837, and two items of expenditure showed important links with the past. In the first "John Dennis was paid £5. 10s. for repairing *Crompton's tomb*", damaged in the collapse of the old church, and Francis Cox was paid £53. 8s. 4d." for Communion Table and rails, *Pallisading Crompton's Tomb*, &c." The railing round of the table-tomb undoubtedly prevented further breakage of this valuable monument, but did nothing to protect it against weather.

The second item of expenditure was £72. 10s. for "Bricks, Lime, etc. and Workmanship in *taking down the old School House and building a New One*." The old school, benefiting from Thomas Alleyne's will since 1558, had either been very close to the old Priory Church and affected by its collapse, or it was on or near the site needed for the new church. The Minute[11] authorising the work had read:

"The Trustees had ordered that the School be pulled down and rebuilt at the place marked out and the foundations set in the churchyard for that purpose, and that a Chamber be made over it, and a Cupola at the Top, under the Inspection of Mr. Shelley, Senr., Mr. John Emery, and Mr. William Barbor, or some of them, and that they shall have power to receive of Mr. Hinckes (Rector) what money is necessary to complete the same".

The original school had been a single storey building, but the Parish took advantage of the rebuilding to add an upstairs room for their Sunday School. The Trustees had shown utter disregard of Trinity College in this matter of the school, and a report by Trinity's Senior Bursar, Mr. Judgson, who visited Stone in 1824[12] to sort out problems relating to the school, revealed some surprising facts. From 1697 the Parish, as well as the College, had been doing repairs to the school; and over the rebuilding "no memorandum or agreement" on the subject had ever been made between the Parish and the College. The failure by the Church authorities to recognise the Trusteeship of Trinity College in matters relating to the Grammar School emphasises the insignificance into which the school had sunk after Thomas Chaloner's period as head. Indeed, the early 18th century showed secondary education at its lowest level.[13]

Meanwhile other interesting things were happening in Stone and to Stone people. *Swynfen Jervis*, while retaining his interests at Meaford, had taken up a legal post in Greenwich, and young *John* left Burton to go to school near his father. The family coachman had already told John that all lawyers were rogues, and that the only career was the sea. The impression went deep, and he and a friend named Strahan ran away to Woolwich. Having hidden for three days on board a ship, and scared the family, he returned home to announce his intention of going to sea. With the help of Lord Anson he joined the navy as an ordinary seaman, and made his first voyage to Jamaica in 1748 at the age of thirteen. His father had given him £20 to start his career, and then refused all further assistance, even to the extent of declining to pay a bill of £20 at the end of two years.[15] The result on Jervis was immediate:

"I immediately changed my mode of living, quitted my mess, lived alone, and took up the ship's allowance which I found quite sufficient; washed and mended my own clothes, made a pair of trousers out of the ticking of my bed, and by these means saved as much money as would redeem my honour."[16]

John Jervis made rapid progress in the navy; after three years he was a midshipman, and on his return from the West Indies in 1754 he was lieutenant. When war broke out with the French he went as first lieutenant with Sir Charles Saunders and *General Wolfe* to Quebec, where, as acting commander of the "Porcupine", Jervis successfully led the transports past Quebec.

Jervis and Wolfe were friends, and on September 11th, the night previous to the assault on the Heights of Abraham, Wolfe went to see Jervis. He told him of a strong presentiment that he would be killed in the following day's battle. He then took from an inner pocket a miniature of a girl to whom he was engaged, and begged that, if his foreboding came true, Jervis would return it personally to Miss Lowther on his return to England; a duty which, unfortunately, became necessary, and which Jervis carried out. Following the capture of Quebec, Jervis served in American waters under Admiral Rodney, until 1763, when he was placed on half-pay. He was at home and virtually unemployed, and was able to spend a lot of time at Meaford.

On July 27th 1765 he had written:

". . . Thursday was bowling day at Stone. Mr. Sneyd, Ld. Vane, Robinson, Lander and young Mills, who by the bye is perpetually drunk, met us there and we spent a jolly day enough".[17]

On September 22nd:
"Thursday, Smith and Wheldon came over to shoot for my London friends. My Bro. and I rode about the *Downs Banks* from seven till nine expecting them; just as we were going home they appeared, knocked down twelve brace before dinner, and were very jolly after."[18]

And on December 1st:
". . . the *Stone hounds* improve very much and I follow them incessantly; this is not the only motive for my staying so much here . . . my clothes are all in tatters."[19]

While John Jervis waited at home for another command, Stone was expectantly waiting for a further development in transport. Not satisfied with the road carriage of his delicate china, *Josiah Wedgwood* had taken up with enthusiasm the idea of transport by canal. On December 30th 1765, a public meeting was held at Wolseley Bridge to consider applying for an Act of Parliament "for making a *Navigable Cut, or Canal, from the River Trent to the River Mersey*."[20] The Act was obtained the following year, and at a meeting in Newcastle on June 3rd 1766, a committee was set up.

The first committee meeting was held at the *Crown in Stone*, on June 10th 1766, when James Brindley was appointed Surveyor General, T. Sparrow Clerk of Works, and Josiah Wedgwood Treasurer. The work of Brindley began the same year, but he died before the whole project was carried out, and it was his brother-in-law, Hugh Henshall, who completed the canal by 1777. The *Stone section was completed in 1771*, and the celebrations on the occasion of the opening were, to say the least, extraordinary:

"The Rejoicings on the Evening of the 12th inft. (November 1771) for the Arrival of the Boats up the canal at Stone, in Staffordshire, ended with great Damage, by the repeated Firing of the Cannon. One of the locks and a bridge fell in, and much damaged another, by which Accident the Boats were not able to return. Damage is computed at £1000."[21]

This canal was, ultimately, to be of great value to Stone. The well-known traveller, Thomas Pennant, seeing boats on the canal to the north-east of the town, remarked: "How would the prophet have been treated who, forty years ago, should have predicted that a vessel of 25 tons would be seen sailing over Stonefield? Yet such is the case."[22]

In February 1769, after six years on half pay, *John Jervis* was recalled to take command of the "Alarm", a frigate of 32 guns. While at Genoa, two Turkish slaves took refuge in one of the ship's boats, wrapping themselves in the British flag. The slaves' owners had them dragged out, and the flag was torn. Jervis was outraged: he demanded that the slaves be brought on board, the official responsible for tearing the flag punished, and an apology made for the incident. Jervis had his way.

Captain John Jervis, painted by Francis Cotes, R.A.
(reproduced by kind permission of the National Portrait Gallery)

PLATE II

Six months later, in March 1770, the "Alarm" was driven ashore in a gale at Marseilles. No lives were lost, but the ship's bottom was almost completely ripped off. Jervis's reputation and his ship were at stake. By superhuman efforts, repairs were carried out in three months, at a total cost of £1415. The Admiralty was so staggered by the speed and the cheapness of the work that Jervis was praised, not blamed, and he returned to England in 1771 with a distinct reputation.

After an extensive tour of the harbours of France and the Baltic, gaining vital information for use later, he took part in the relief of Gibraltar in 1782, and in the same year took command of the "Foudroyant" of 74 guns, in the fleet of Admiral Barrington. On the night of April 20th, off Brest, in rough weather, the "Foudroyant" brought the French ship "Pégase", of 74 guns and 700 men, to a close action which soon forced the Frenchman to surrender. Admiral Barrington wrote of this action: "My pen is not equal to the praise that is due to the good conduct, bravery and discipline of Captain Jervis, his Officers and Seamen on this occasion." Jervis had not lost a man in the engagement. He was made a Knight of the Bath and then, later in the year, married his cousin Martha Parker.

Between 1783 and 1793 he was a member of Parliament, but confined himself to naval matters, serving at sea between these parliamentary interludes, with the rank of Rear-admiral. Promoted Vice-Admiral in November 1793 he took an expedition to the West Indies, with Sir Charles Grey as his military coadjutor. Such was the harmony between the leaders, as well as the speed and vigour of the operation that between the beginning of February and the end of April 1794, Martinique, Santa Lucia and Guadeloupe had been captured, and England was in possession of the Windward Isles. On his return "the Common Council held in the Chamber of the Guildhall of the City of London on Thursday, the 27th May 1794, resolved unanimously that the *Freedom of the City* be presented to Sir John Jervis, K.B., . . ."

In 1795 Jervis took command of the Mediterranean Fleet, then the most important post in the navy, because of events in France. With the rise of Napoleon, the former enemies of France had hastened to make peace, and England was left without an ally. Jervis hurried out to the Mediterranean to face innumerable difficulties: ships desperate for stores, crews riddled with fever and scurvy; corruption in the dockyards at home; ship's complements woefully short; the navy's bases in the Mediterranean becoming increasingly difficult to hold. Jervis was the man for the post; he was a splendid disciplinarian, and yet he had the greatest care for the health of his men, and for their efforts. He inspired confidence and enthusiasm in all serving under him, so thoroughly was he acquainted with every branch of seamanship. And in his fleet were a number of young officers destined for fame, among them Nelson, Collingwood and Hood.

By the end of 1796 Jervis's fleet had been forced to leave the Mediterranean, and to make its way towards England through repeated hurricanes, so that by the time he reached Lisbon four ships had gone, and no battle been fought. Yet Jervis remained immovably firm. Stores and provisions materialised somehow, repairs went steadily ahead; men were conjured up to make up the shortage of crews. Then advice came from England on the 16th of December that the French fleet had got out of Brest, and that the Spanish fleet had left Toulon. The aim was for these two fleets to unite, and pave the way for a landing in Ireland as a preliminary to the invasion of England.

On January 18th 1797 Jervis felt obliged to sail with what ships he had, and he cruised with ten ships off *Cape St. Vincent*. On February 6th Parker joined him with further ships, Nelson rejoined him a week later, and the battered fleet was increased to fifteen ships. On the day of Nelson's return, news had come that the Spanish fleet was advancing northwards. England's position was now desperate, and Jervis set off in pursuit. Throughout the night of the 13th he remained awake; he made his will, and pondered over the chance which, at the age of sixty-two, fate had at last given him.

Long before daybreak he was pacing the quarter-deck, in his usual stern silence. The grey dawn showed his fleet in "admirable close order". He commended them, and added the message: "A victory is very essential to England at this moment"[23] As the light improved the leading Spanish ships were sighted:

"There are eight sail-of-the-line, Sir John", reported Calder, the captain of the fleet.

"Very well, sir", the admiral replied.

"There are twenty sail-of-the-line . . . twenty-five . . ." said Calder, as the ships were gradually counted. "There are twenty-seven sail, Sir John", he said, remarking at the same time upon the disparity between the English and Spanish fleets.

"Enough, sir", Jervis testily replied, "No more of that. The die is cast, and if there are fifty sail, I will go through them".[24]

This was not bravado. For over a year Jervis had moulded his fleet, and it bore no resemblance to the ill-disciplined, fever-ridden body which had so worried him when he took command. The Spaniards were seen to be in two divisions, and the attack was first directed against the smaller leeward division, but this section soon fled. Jervis then made the signal to tack in succession and fall upon the Spanish windward division. The Spanish ships were faster, and had the British ships continued to tack in succession, might well have escaped. *Nelson*, in the third ship from the rear, left the line, and threw himself across the path of the leading Spaniard. Jervis immediately ordered the last ship in the line, the "Excellent", to support Nelson's "Captain", and the "Culloden" which had moved out with him. Nelson related afterwards that when the two ships swung out of line, Calder pointed out to Sir John that they had not followed the prescribed order of attack. Jervis replied: "I will not have them recalled. I put my faith in those two ships".

By five in the afternoon, two Spanish ships of 112 guns each, one of 84 and one of 74 were captured; the rest, many of them wrecks, took shelter in Cadiz and were blockaded by the admiral. By this great victory the threatened invasion by joint fleets of Spain and France no longer caused anxiety; moreover the skill and disciplinarian powers of Jervis, aided by the valour of Nelson, brought hope for the future.

The news of the *victory* reached London on the afternoon of Saturday, March 3rd, and that same evening the House of Commons, by acclamation, passed a vote of thanks to Jervis. A pension of £3,000 was voted on Jervis, and Nelson was made Knight of the Bath. The King had previously nominated Jervis for a peerage in reward for earlier services; the victory gave him an independent claim. He was gazetted at one step to *an earldom*, the King himself choosing the title of *St. Vincent*, which he signed for the first time on July 15th.

> "My dear Brother,
>   His Majesty fixed on St. Vincent, but Baron Jervis of Meaford is the foundation stone of all, and I cannot describe the happiness I feel in deriving from a beautiful spot where I have passed many delightful hours.
>   St. Vincent,
> Ville de Paris at anchor before Cadiz, 15th July 1797."

Soon after the victory of Cape St. Vincent, widespread mutinies broke out among the English sailors at Spithead and the Nore, brought about by bad conditions, wretched food, irregular pay and harsh treatment. St. Vincent's squadron, continuing to blockade Cadiz was "the only part of His Majesty's fleet to be relied on", and its loyalty was partly due to the stern discipline which he enforced, and partly to his efforts to ensure the men's health and comfort. St. Vincent's ships were deperately in need of repair, but necessity compelled him to keep them at sea, and as disaffected ships came out from England, mutiny broke out in his too. The old admiral, now 63, dealt with mutiny quickly, ruthlessly and successfully, but he was suffering severely from strain, and wrote thus from the "Ville de Paris", off Cadiz, on April 30th 1798:

> "My health having given way through the extensive fatigues of mind and body I have gone through the two years and eight months past . . . I have applied to be relieved, and probably shall be in England during the summer. I have not yet apprised Lady St. Vincent of this measure, therefore pray confine it to the *Bow Parlour*.[25] My plan is to go to Bath the moment I arrive at Spithead, and to ramble about the country until winter, taking Stone in my tour."[26]

With St. Vincent off Cadiz was another Stone hero: *Thomas Oldfield*, third son of Humphrey Oldfield, an officer in the Marines, who was born at *Stone* on June 21st 1756. Accompanying his father to America in 1774, he served as a volunteer at Bunker's Hill at the beginning of the American War of Independence. He served in many of the campaigns of this war, and was eventually taken prisoner with Lord Cornwallis at the capitulation of Yorktown.

At the termination of the American War, Oldfield returned to England to take up his commission in the marines, then went out to the West Indies in the "Sceptre" from 1778 to 1795. It was in 1797 that he embarked on board the "Theseus", 74 guns, and joined St. Vincent's squadron blockading Cadiz. This ship was for a time the flagship of Nelson, then a rear-admiral, and after the second bombardment of Cadiz, Oldfield commanded the marines in Nelson's unsuccessful attack upon the island of Tenneriffe, the action in which Nelson lost his arm. Later Oldfield served with Nelson, who flew his flag in the "Vanguard", at the Battle of the Nile, and led the attack on the French fleet. Early in 1799 the "Theseus" sailed to join Sir Sidney Smith off the coast of Syria, and Oldfield took part in the defence of St. Jean d'Arc. On April 7th, at daybreak, a sortie in three columns was made against the French, Oldfield leading the centre column. In this action he was mortally wounded. The French general Berthier records that Oldfield was dead when he arrived at H.Q., and continues. "His sword, to which he had done so much honour, was also honoured after his death ... He was buried among us, and he has carried with him to the grave the esteem of the French army." His gallant conduct was eulogised in the official dispatch of Sir Sidney Smith, and Napoleon, when on passage to St. Helena, spoke of *Oldfield's gallantry* to the marine officers on board the "Northumbria".

Meanwhile, at home, the progress in road transport continued, and by the end of the century all the principal roads serving Stone had been turnpiked. A renewal of the *Lichfield to Stone* Act in 1743 stipulated that "no toll gate must be nearer to Stone than 9 miles".[27] The *Eccleshall to Stone road* had been turnpiked in 1771, but the demands upon it were such that in 1792 a petition was presented to the House of Commons "that a road from a place called *Walton*, in Stone, to *Eccleshall*, in the said county, is in many places ruinous, narrow and incommodious, and cannot be effectually amended, widened and kept in Repair by the ordinary Course of Law: And therefore praying That leave be given to bring in a Bill for continuing the said Act (of 1771) . . .and that provision may be made in the said Bill for repairing and widening the said road from Walton to Eccleshall."[28]

In 1793 the Trustees of the *Stone to Uttoxeter turnpike* undertook the making of an entirely new length of road: "Petition for setting out and making a new Road from the Westwardly Part of *Hardiwick Heath* to the Wolseley Bridge Turnpike Road in the *village of Stoke* in the Parish of Stone."[29] The old road thus replaced is crossed by the new road at the foot of Slowgreaves Bank: it can still be seen skirting the hill to work round to the east of Little Stoke Farm.

In 1771 an Act was passed allowing turnpikes along the road from *Stone to Lane End (or Longton)*, this being our present Old Road, and for long known as the Cheadle Turnpike Road; toll gates were set up at the bottom of Old Rd. in Stone, and at Hobbergate. The present road from *Walton to Aston and Stafford* was a turnpike road by 1761.

The 5th Viscount Torrington has left us an account of a night's stay in Stone in 1792:

"As the rain now return'd with violence I trotted briskly along, by the side of the navigation, to the end of the town of Stone, where I re-hovel'd for an hour; when, finding no cessation of rain, I ventured out to take a peep at the inn, and to this, liking the appearance, I removed my quarters. . . . *The Crown* appear'd to be a good house, with symptons of civility, where, taking possession of a good parlour (with a good fire, June 29th) I ordered dinner, and then read the London newspapers with great avidity, after my long ride. . . . I was much entertained from my window, with the sight of four lusty Irish gentlemen coming forth from a hackney post-chaise with 4 horses; and afterwards being repack'd in another; instead of going in two chaises, drawn by two horses each; which I should have thought a pleasanter way of travelling."[30]

The proprietor of the Crown at this time was *Mr. Lillyman*, who was also postmaster of Stone. The hotel was for a long period the posting-house, with the letter-box in one of the bow fronts of the building. Shortly before Mr. Lillyman became postmaster the *first mail coach* along the Chester road came through Stone (in 1785), and John Carey[31] records in 1795 that mail coaches were calling at the *Crown*.

Roads were now improved and more travelling was done, but the dangers of bad roads were now replaced by other dangers. The "Red Lion" inn on the Milwich road is reputed to have been a haunt of highwaymen: there were robbers on the Newcastle road too, as this report of 1763 showed:

"A few days ago, Mr. Taton, Rider to Messrs. Reynold and Dawson of Leeds, was robbed between *Stone* and *Newcastle* of £11 and his watch by a Footpad, who clapp'd a Pistol to his Side, and afterwards cut the Girths of his Saddle."[32]

In 1799 there was a serious accident at *Tittensor*, when "on Tuesday morning (8th October), about half-past seven o'clock, the *"Balloon" coach* from Liverpool to Birmingham, by some accident, was overturned into the River Trent at Tittensor . . . which is much swelled by the late incessant rains. There were six inside and three outside passengers, besides two coachmen, the regular driver being ill on the roof when the coach fell; and we are sorry to add that three of the inside passengers were unfortunately drowned . . ."[33]

In this same year of 1799 *Darlaston Bridge* was rebuilt,[34] *Strongford Bridge* having been rebuilt six years previously.

The *canal* was also bringing great activity to the town. The head office of the Canal Company was at Westbridge House,[35] Stone, where to reduce the risk of fire all the office shelves were of slate. A notice, issued from the Navigation Office, Stone, by Hugh Henshall & Co. informed the public that the whole of the Navigation, 99 miles in length, was now completed. Regular stage-boats were arranged between the various places on the route of the canal, and the table of prices showed an enormous reduction of cost compared with that for land carriage, e.g. between Chester and Wolverhampton, £1. 15s. per ton as against £3. 10s. and between Manchester and Newark, £2 per ton as against £5. 6s. 8d.

The "Topographer" in 1789 ascribed much of Stone's progress to the canal:

"The town is in a much more flourishing state than formerly, owing to the great navigation that passes by it. It consists of one principal street, which is now a pretty good one, with a new market place, and one of the leading inns upon this extensive road. . . . Tho' the expence attending this astonishing work (the canal) was enormous, so as to promise little or no profit to the adventurers, yet in a few years after it was finished, I saw the smile of hope brighten every countenance; new buildings and new streets spring up in so many parts of Staffordshire, where it passes, the poor no longer on the bread of poverty, and the rich grow daily richer. The market town of *Stone* in particular soon felt this comfortable change, which from a poor insignificant place is now grown neat and handsome in its buildings, and, from its wharfs and busy traffic, wears the lively aspect of a little sea-port."[36]

A new road had been cut from near the present Mansion House, to form a direct approach to High Street. This new Lichfield St. almost put an end to the use by vehicles of the old King's highway, and encroachment upon Crown St. or, as it was once called Back Lane, resulted in this part of the highway being cut in two, with only a footpath joining the two portions. Only in the latter half of the 20th century has this part of the original highway been re-opened to through traffic.

The Topographer's remarks about poverty in 1789 were in marked contrast with the view of Arthur Young during his northern tour in 1770:

"Poor rates 1s. 6d. in the pound. Idleness is the chief employment of the women and children. All drink tea and flie to the parish for relief, at the very time that even a woman for washing is not to be had. By many accounts I received of the poor in this neighbourhood, I apprehend the rates are burthened for the spreading (of) laziness, drunkenness, tea-drinking and debauchery—the general effect of them, indeed, all over the country."[37]

In 1792 an Act of Parliament was obtained "for Providing a *Workhouse* for the Reception of the poor of the *Parish of Stone* . . . and for Regulating and employing the Poor therein." By this Act 42 Directors and Guardians were appointed; preliminary meetings were held "at the School-house in the churchyard in Stone", and the advice of John Jervis was sought. He it was, indeed, who had helped to obtain the Act, which was designed to replace the old 17th century thatched workhouse; Jervis was living at Rochetts in Essex, and he obtained for the Guardians the "plans of Romford (Essex) Workhouse, and the Rules and Orders therein established."

On July 13th 1792 the Guardians accepted the tender of Benjamin Wyatt and William Emery for erecting a workhouse for £1190; on April 1st 1793 land for the building was given by the Marquis of Stafford, and work went on apace. George Henney, and Elizabeth his wife, were appointed to be Governor and Matron.

This new workhouse was so great an improvement that it drew comment in the "Gentlemen's Magazine" in 1794:

"A newly-erected workhouse at the south-west angle of the town, both for its size and convenience, merits public notice."[38]

NOTES AND REFERENCES

1. N.S. Field Club Trans. vol. 45 (1910–11) p. 210; Field's Note Book, 5, fo. 14; and the Parish Registers.
2. N.S. Field Club Trans. vol. 35 (1900–01) p. 162.
3. House of Commons Journal, vol. xxvi, p. 533 (24 January 1753).
4. Minute Book of the Rebuilding, Min. no. 2 (31 July 1753).
5. ibid. Min. no. 4 (25 September 1753).
6. ibid. Min. no. 27 (27 December 1754). "The Rowe" was part of what is now Church St.
7. ibid. Min. no. 61 (1 February 1757).
8. ibid. Min. no. 51 (13 April 1756).
9. Church Registers.
10. For detailed accounts see Bowers & Clough: Researches into the History of Stone, 1928.
11. Minute Book: Min. no. 90 (26 September 1758).
12. Trinity College Muniments: Stone School: Box 33 (I.b.) See Plate 13 for illustration of this rebuilt school.
13. S. J. Curtis: History of Education in Great Britain, 1948, p. 51.
14. O. A. Sherrard: Life of Lord St. Vincent, pp. 29–30.
15. Brenton: Life of Earl St. Vincent, I.20; and J. S. Tucker: Memoirs of Earl St. Vincent, I. 10.
16. O. A. Sherrard: op. cit. p. 31.
17. British Museum: Add. Mss. 29914, f. 2.
18. ibid. f. 9.
19. ibid. f. 15.
20. 6 Geo. III. c. 96.
21. St. James' Chronicle or British Evening Post, from Tuesday Nov. 26th to Thursday Nov. 28th. 1771.
22. The Journey from Chester to London, 1782, p. 50.
23. O. A. Sherrard: op. cit. pp. 97–103.
24. Taprell Dorling (Taffrail): Men o' War, p. 14.
25. The Bow Parlour: the Earl's favourite sitting-room at Meaford.
26. Meaford Papers.
27. S.H.C. 1934, p. 44.
28. House of Commons Journal, vol. xlvii, p. 463 (1 March 1792).
29. House of Commons Journal, vol. xlviii, p. 93 (23 January 1793) and the Lord Harrowby Mss.
30. The Torrington Diaries, 1936, pp. 130–131 (Tours of the Hon. John Byng, afterwards 5th Viscount Torrington).
31. New Itinerary, p. 162.
32. Lloyd (London) Evening Post, Nov. 16–18, 1763, no. 991 (Salt Ms. 2062, v.).
33. Staffordshire Advertiser, 12 October 1799.
34. S.H.C. 1934, p. 89.
35. Now demolished: it stood near the present Westbridge Park entrance gates.
36. The Topographer, June 1789, pp. 116–124.
37. Arthur Young: Six Months Tour through the North of England, vol. III., pp. 258 f.
38. Gentlemen's Magazine Library, vol. 23, edited by G. L. Gomme, F.S.A., London, 1899, p. 23; 1794, Pt. II. pp. 1077–1081.

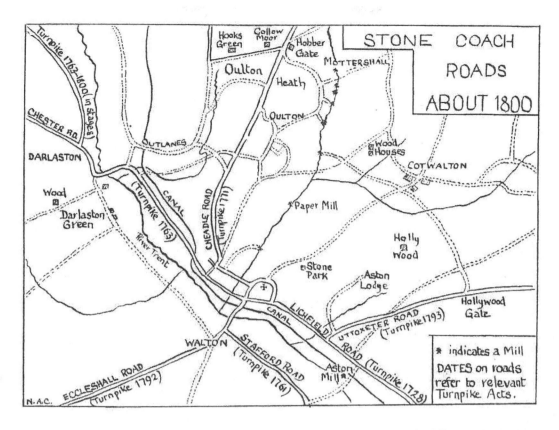

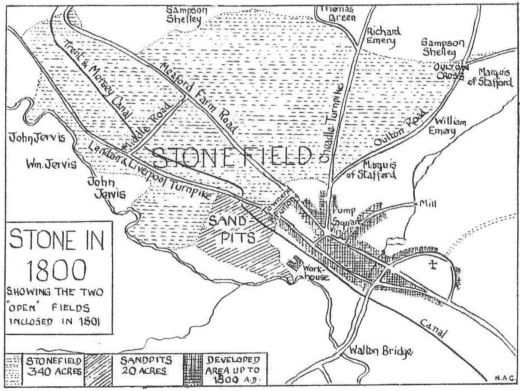

PLATE 12

CHAPTER *10*

INTO THE NINETEENTH CENTURY

In common with the rest of the country, there was no lack of enthusiasm in Stone to raise "reserve" forces for the defence of England against the threats of the French under Napoleon. In 1794 Earl Gower, later Duke of Sutherland, had raised the "Staffordshire Regiment of Gentlemen and Yeomanry", and four years later *George Steedman of Cold Meece* raised the Stone and Eccleshall squadron of Volunteer Cavalry. The uniform was a red jacket with yellow facings, white waistcoat, white leather breeches, military boots, helmet with bear-skin crest and feather at the side. The arms consisted of sword and pistol, and the belts were of pipe-clayed yellow. So troublous were the times in which the squadron was formed that exercises took place twice weekly. In 1814, when the country was no longer in danger, the troop was disbanded.

There was a company of Volunteers in 1800, who, on June 4th of that year joined with the local cavalry to fire "three excellent vollies in honour of His Majesty's birthday, and afterwards dined together at the Crown Inn."[1] In 1803 the Stone and Sandon Company of Loyal Volunteers was raised by Major R. W. Topp (retired from the 120th Regt. of Foot) and Col. W. Sneyd, to the number of 360.

A medal presented by Major Topp has been preserved: a silver engraved medal, $2\frac{5}{8}$ inches in diameter, with broad raised rim, inscribed thus:

"Obverse: A volunteer firing at a circular target.
Above: STONE. Below: VOLUNTEERS.
Reverse: Ball firing, a reward for skill from
Major R. W. Topp, September 1807;
two olive branches below."[2]

To many other people in the Stone district, especially the poor, the period of the Napoleonic wars was one of great hardship. Prices rose at an alarming rate, without any rise in wages. In 1795 wheat was around 200s. a quarter as a result of cornfactors monopolising supplies. In 1800, following a bad harvest the previous year, butter was up to 16d a pound, bacon 14d., cheese 10d., and eggs 2d. each.[3] With the wages of many labourers still less than 10s, a week, there was much suffering and unhappiness.

In the meantime, *Earl St. Vincent's* wish to be relieved of his heavy responsibilities at the end of April 1798 was not to be granted. On May 19th a momentous letter came from the Admiralty: "The appearance of a British fleet in the Mediterranean is a condition upon which the fate of Europe may be said to depend." St. Vincent did not hesitate: he sent his own loyal ships with Nelson; he himself continued to hold the Spanish fleet in check with a fresh lot of ships from England, seething with discontent. Almost immediately a request for a court-martial came from the "Marlborough", where mutiny had broken out. A seaman was found guilty, and next morning St. Vincent ordered him to be hanged by the crew of his own ship. The fleet relaxed into submission: St. Vincent remarked, "Discipline is preserved."

He did his best to get rid of those officers upon whom he could not rely, and he himself worked even harder on behalf of the men, improving their standards and their morale. His task was made easier by Nelson's victory of the Nile. Writing from Gibraltar on December 13th he wrote that he was "straining every nerve" in co-operating with Lord Nelson; then went on to express his pleasure that "the southern frontier of Meaford was soon to be extended", and continued with advice on health. "I believe that early rising, short diet and living much in the air is now more efficacious than even the water (i.e. spa water), but as you have a good turnpike road between Meaford and Buxton, it is certainly wise to pay an annual visit there in the driest season you can find."

But St. Vincent's health was getting worse, and on June 17th 1799 he resigned his command. He retired to his home at Rochetts in Essex to recuperate, and from there went to Bath in the care of Dr. Baird. The Admiralty, in desperate need of his services, sought the doctor's consent for his return, but Baird was adamant in his refusal. However, private consultations took place in the doctor's absence, and St. Vincent suddenly announced that he was off to sea. "The King and the Government require it, and the discipline of the Navy demands it", he said. "It is of no consequence to me whether I die afloat or ashore. The die is cast." On April 26th 1800 St. Vincent took command of the Channel Fleet, and set to work once more to build a fleet to his standard, always caring for the food and clothing of his men. Ignoring ill-health, he commenced the blockade of Brest, with but few hours' sleep, working and scheming incessantly for his fleet, yet longing for the peace of his old home. He wrote from the "Ville de Paris" off Brest on June 15th 1800:

"I shall be happy to renew my acquaintance with every particle of the environs of the delightful spot of my nativity, to view your improvements in *Stone Field*, and embrace my sister and you, when this Trojan war is at an end."[4]

And from the same ship in Torbay on October 7th 1800:

"My dear Brother,

Young Simpkin is under my protection & Captain Harvey of the "Triumph" says he will do . . . Bargain for the *Outlanes* it matters not at what price, and tell Vernon to keep out the Squire of Darlaston".[5]

The *Earl* loved Meaford, where his brother William lived, and where the full range of country produce was at his disposal, and where, in the kitchen garden, he would indulge his fondness for gooseberries and raw parsley. No smoking was permitted in the house at Meaford, but on a knoll, about 500 yards away, a smoking house was built for the use of William Jervis and his guests; four sycamore trees were planted at the four corners, and although the little house has gone, the stunted sycamores remain.[6]

Despite his toughness, St. Vincent was compelled, before 1800 was out, to command the Channel Fleet from ashore at Tor Abbey, and on February 3rd 1801 he resigned his command. After much persuasion he accepted the post of *First Lord of the Admiralty*, and immediately he infused a greater efficiency into naval administration, and set up a Commission of Inquiry to clear out corruption.

In October of 1805 Nelson gained his great victory of Trafalgar, and died in the hour of triumph. With Nelson dead, no one but St. Vincent could inspire confidence among the public, and so, when turned seventy, he once again accepted command of the Channel Fleet. He shouldered the old duties and the old fatigues, though age pressed so heavily that he could not even write with ease. Then, in 1807, he hauled down his flag for the last time, and paid his final visit to the House of Lords in 1810, when Sheridan referred to "his triple laurel, over the enemy, the mutineer and the corrupt."

His wife died in 1816 and was buried at Caverswall. The Earl lived to the age of 88, paying frequent visits to his sister Mary (Mrs. Ricketts) at Meaford. When he died on March 13th 1823, his will instructed that no display of pomp should appear at his funeral, which took place at Stone on March 26th. His body was laid to rest in the family mausoleum, where his father Swynfen had been buried in 1771, his mother in 1784, and his elder brother William in 1813.

At the west end of the parish church is a memorial tablet on which a long inscription sets out the Earl's career, and the tablet is surmounted by a bust of the Earl, the work of Sir Francis Chantrey. In 1823 a monument was erected to the Earl in St. Paul's Cathedral, and in more recent times Captain Taprell Dorling has written this tribute:

"He raised the British navy from a condition of mediocrity to a state of high discipline and fighting efficiency, the like of which the world had never previously known. . . . He gave Nelson his first independent command, and forged the weapon which enabled that greatest of British seamen to win this crowning triumph of Trafalgar. Nelson and his men fought the battle; the rugged old Earl had created the fleet."[7]

The town for which St. Vincent had such affection was, in 1801, a prosperous and growing little town of 1500 people. *Francis Joule*, in 1758, was brewing in the town on the site of an earlier brewery believed to have been established in the 17th century. The business was transferred in 1818 by Francis and Sarah his wife to their son, *John*, the founder of the firm which, until very recently, bore his name. *William Dixon* was recorded in 1787[8] as a shoe manufacturer, and *Moses Hassels* and *William Wardell* both as ribbon manufacturers.

In 1797 Mr. Joule was advertising for a "Maltster: a man who perfectly understands the business. . . . None need apply but such as may be well recommended."[9] The following year "*John Hincks, Tallow-Chandler, Stone,* Respectfully informs the Shopkeepers and Inhabitants of Stafford and its vicinity, that he has taken a Shop near the "Vine Inn", where he continues to sell Candles on the same liberal terms he has hitherto done."[10]

Games and sports played a large part in the life of the people at the turn of the century, though the emphasis was more on cruelty than our present age would tolerate. Bull- and bear-baiting, dog- and cock-fighting were some of the attractions for the people who flocked into the town at the time of fairs or the wakes. Bulls were baited in Pump Square (now known as Granville Square), on the spot where the County Library (formerly the Market Hall) now stands, at the junction of Stafford St. and Lichfield St. (where the "Four Crosses" inn later stood) and in Church St. Bears were baited behind what was the "Unicorn" hotel and is now shop development, in fact where the cattle markets are held. Baiting often took place three times a day, a small entrance fee being paid for each dog, the owner of the one which held the bull (or bear) for the longest period receiving the prize, usually a leg of mutton or a copper kettle. Pits for cock-fighting were in Cross St. and in the Crown Meadow. Here is a typical notice, dated 1751:

"COCK FIGHTING

"This is to give notice that there is to be fought a Main of Cocks between the Gentlemen of Derbyshire and Staffordshire, at *the Crown Inn, in Stone*, for Ten Guineas a Battle, and Sixty the Main. To weigh 27 Cocks on each Side, and Ten for Bye Battles, upon Wednesday, the 20th March next, and the two following days."[11]

The peace of the town was kept by *constables* elected annually by the towns-folk. Offenders against the law were placed in the pillory or stocks. The pillory was in the Market Square, near the old Butter Market,[12] and the last man stood in it in 1848. There was a set of stocks at the old *Walton Corner*, near the original *Lamb Inn*, which, until its demolition, was the end building of Elm Terrace. In 1810 the Overseers of the Poor paid 2 shillings for locks for these stocks. The last set of stocks are believed to have been made by *Isaac Dutton* who, either as a joke, or maybe through excessive exuberance, was the first to be placed in them. Dutton was a wheelwright in Mill St. at least from 1835 to 1851,[13] most probably on the same site as the present premises of Messrs. Price and Stubbs. At the Walton end of the bridge over the Trent, at the side where the footbridge now is, was the *pinfold*, in which straying animals were kept until claimed. On February 19th 1811 James Mills was paid 5 shillings "for mending Pinfold Gate at Style at Bridge End."[14] There was also a pinfold or pound near the (present) Church St. railway crossing.

One of the favourite games of the people was "prison bars",[15] and they also played "tip-cat", the "cats" being made of tips of horn, or of box or yew. Some of the games were played for considerable sums of money. "Hare and hounds" was played on winter nights, the hares being provided with horns, which were blown at frequent intervals.

Each day the "prentice bell' or rising bell was rung at the Parish Church, on weekdays at 6 a.m., and on Sundays at 7 a.m., after which the day of the month was tolled. The curfew rang each night, from Lady-day to Michaelmas at 8 o'clock, and for the other six months an hour earlier. On Sundays at one o'clock in the afternoon, a bell was rung for ten minutes; it was called the "parson's bell", but no-one seems to know why it was so-called or what its purpose was. These ringing customs were discontinued after the abolition of Church Rates in 1868.

To *Stone* in 1781 came a struggling young doctor named *Henry de Wint*. The de Wints were a prosperous family of Dutch merchants, and Henry belonged to a branch of the family living in America, part of his youth being spent in New York. While studying medicine in London, and living on an allowance from America, Henry de Wint became engaged to a Miss Watson, a Scottish girl whose father had emptied his purse and nearly lost his head in the cause of Bonnie Prince Charlie. Henry did not mind the girl's poverty, though his marriage to her in 1773 upset the plans which his father had made for the future. In his letters home Henry took care not to say that he had a wife, but the fact became known, and his father disinherited him. Henry now had a wife and two children to support, and he did what he could to build up a practice near Cardiff. The life there did not suit him, and in 1781 he came to *Stone*, where success of a modest kind was won. At Stone ten more children were born, and there, *in a house adjoining the Crown Hotel*,[16] *Peter*, who was the fourth son, was born on *January 21st 1784*.

From childhood Peter was devoted to drawing, and he soon expressed a desire to become an artist. Whilst at school, he drew not only for his own amusement, but tried his best to teach his school fellows to sketch. He wandered alone through the countryside, making drawings of anything that caught his eye, and one of his early efforts was a water colour of Old Hilderstone Hall. After a time Peter won his father's consent to be an artist, and took lessons from a Mr. Rogers at Stafford. Later, in 1802, he was taken by coach to London, and apprenticed to the famous mezzo-tinter and portrait painter, John Raphael Smith. He went to live in Covent Garden, at a time when there was a wealth of artists: Samuel Prout and David Cox had been born in 1783; John S. Cotman in 1782, Turner and Gurtin in 1775, and Constable in 1776. A fellow apprentice with Peter was William Hilton, who was to find fame later as an R.A., and a painter of historical and biblical subjects. A friendship grew up between these two boys which was to endure for the rest of their lives.

Raphael Smith was a stern and exacting task-master. The terms set forth in the old parchment of apprenticeship had to be carried out to the letter, and the younger boy, shy and sensitive, rebelled and ran away to his home in Lincoln. Peter was the only one who knew of the truant's whereabouts, and he refused to betray the secret to his master. Smith was not one to be toyed with, and he hauled his truculent pupil before a magistrate. Peter remained silent even under the questioning of the law. There was but one way left to deal with refractory apprentices, and Peter was sent to prison. There he remained, until news of his plight reached Lincoln. Hilton hastened back to London, and surrendered himself to his master, thereby setting his friend at liberty. The two boys then got back to work and the incident was forgotten.

In 1806, barely four years after signing the indentures, Raphael Smith terminated the existing agreement with his pupil. A new contract was drawn up with Doctor de Wint, signed and dated May 17th 1806. whereby Peter, now 22, agreed to paint nine pictures in oils, all to be landscapes, and to be delivered into the hands of "and to be the absolute property of the said Raphael John Smith", by the end of the first year. A further nine pictures were to be delivered by the end of the second year. An entry on the back of this old agreement records the receipt from Mr. de Wint "of all the pictures . . . in this agreement except a picture of a Farm House on the Paddington Canal, now in the British Institution, May 2nd 1808." A year before this *Peter de Wint* was seen for the first time at the Royal Academy, his pictures being a view of "Trentham" and one of "Matlock High Tor."

De Wint and Hilton continued their associations, and after spending a period at the latter's home at Lincoln, the pair set up for themselves in London. It was during his first visit to Lincoln that de Wint met Harriet Hilton, his friend's sister, then fifteen years of age. The foundation was laid for an enduring love between them, and on June 16th 1810 they were married. Although he continued to work with Hilton in London during the winter time, he spent most of the summers at Lincoln with his wife and her family, varied only by visits to the country houses of his pupils, and to carry out commissions for portraits. After the birth of their only child, a daughter, in 1811, his wife's health caused him much uneasiness, and he was unwilling to be away from her for long.

He never cared to go abroad to paint foreign scenery, but maintained his great love for the English landscape. He was a great admirer of the Thames, and had many studies of the Trent; he loved Ludlow and Bridgnorth, Lancaster, Tintern, Caernarvon and Conway. He also did drawings for books, and Ormerod's History of Cheshire has sixteen illustrations by de Wint.

He became not only one of the finest water-colourists of the English school, but also an admirable worker in oils. In his last years the strain of a lifetime of hard work began to tell on his constitution. He became irritable, and suffered recurring attacks of bronchitis which hastened his death. This occurred on June 30th 1849, at the age of sixty-five.

There is not in Staffordshire a representative collection of Peter de Wint's work, although in 1940 the National Art Collection Fund presented to the City of Stoke-on-Trent one of his drawings, "A View of the Thames". Both the South Kensington Museum and the National Gallery have good examples of his work, and the *Usher Art Gallery at Lincoln*[17] has a collection of his works as well as a display of relics connected with de Wint and his family.[18]

NOTES AND REFERENCES

1. Staffordshire Advertiser, 7 June 1800.
2. D. Hasting Irwin: War Medals and Decorations, 1588–1910 (4th edition) p. 399.
3. Parish Registers and N.S. Field Club Trans. vol. xlv (1910–11) p. 210.
4. Meaford Papers.
5. Meaford Papers, and quoted in Taffrail: Men o' War, p. 52.
6. Taffrail: op. cit. p. 67. The trees are near Meaford Road, at the corner of the road down to Meaford Old Hall Farm and the "watery lanes".
7. Taffrail: op. cit. p. 66.
8. Directory of the Principal Merchants and Manufacturers, being a supplement to William Tunnicliff's "Topographical Survey of the Counties of Stafford, Chester and Lancaster", Nantwich, 1787.
9. Staffordshire Advertiser, 26 January 1797.
10. ibid. 26 January 1797.
11. J. R. Booth: Stone: Links with the Past, p. 38.
12. See plate 10. The Butter Market was replaced by the Market Hall, now converted to a County Branch Library.
13. Staffordshire Directories, various. (Guildhall Library, London).
14. Accounts of the Overseers of the Poor.
15. see Arnold Bennett: Old Wives Tale, p. 209, for an account of this game as played in the Potteries.
16. See Plate 10. The house is now Boots the Chemists.
17. This gallery publishes an excellent catalogue of the De Wint Collection.
18. See the Dictionary of National Biography and notes collected by the late W. H. Bowers (Stone Guardian, 2 July 1949).

Portion of the codicil to the Will of Thomas Alleyne, expressing his intention
to found three Grammar Schools.
(by permission of the Central Registry, Somerset House)

The Grammar School in the Parish Churchyard, about 1800.
(by kind permission of the Trustees of the William Salt Library, Stafford)

PLATE 13

CHAPTER 11

THE TOWN DEVELOPS

In spite of the developments in the centre of Stone which had slowly followed the break-up of the Priory lands, such as the extension of the High St. towards the church and the opening of Lichfield St., the area to the north-west of the town remained virtually unchanged. This land, from the *Town-end Furlong* (now Margaret St.) to Oulton Cross and round in a great sweep almost to Meaford, then along the Trent to our present Trent hospital, was still open. This area comprised the *Sandpits* and *Stonefield*, with a total, in two great fields, of 360 acres, still being cultivated, by agreement, in strips, as it had been since mediaeval times. In other parts of the district farms were self-contained, and some were beginning to try the new ideas in farming which characterised this period. Arthur Young visited the district in 1770 and has left us much information about agriculture. One farm of 400 acres (150 arable and 250 grass) employed 3 men servants and 6 labourers. The stock consisted of 36 cows, 30 young cattle, 12 fatting beasts, 50 sheep and 12 horses.

The chief manure being used on the land was *marl*, at 120 loads (of 25 cwt.) per acre, and the large number of "old marl-pits" in the area remain as proof of this; only a little lime was being used. An acre was considered sufficient for the summer feed of one cow; winter feed was hay and straw; and the average yield from one of the long-horned cattle then being kept was 5 gallons a day.

In harvest-time a labourer was paid 1s. 6d. a day; in haytime 1s. 2d. a day, and the remainder of the year 1s. a day, and in each case beer was supplied as an addition to these wages. A woman working in harvest-time received 7d. a day, and beer. In addition to his board, a man was paid 5s. per 120 loads for filling the marl cart. The "first" man on a farm was paid £8 a year plus his board and washing, which were reckoned to be worth £6. 10s. a year.

A waggon cost £20, a cart £12, a plough 14s., a harrow 18s., a scythe 3s. 6d. and a spade 3s. 6d.; shoeing a horse cost 1s. 4d. Bricks were 11s. 6d. a thousand, and tiles 17s.; a mason and a carpenter were each paid 1s. 6d. a day, and a thatcher 1s. a day and board.[1] An *old Stone account book of 1771*[2] confirms Young's evidence, for in this book a farm hand received £7 a year and a pair of shoes.

New methods in farming being clearly impossible on open fields, it was inevitable that a demand should come for inclosure, and the rather varied and casual methods of achieving this in the past now gave way to inclosure by Act of Parliament. The following notice appeared in the "Staffordshire Advertiser" on July 29th 1797:

"INCLOSURE OF STONE FIELD.

"The Landowners and Persons having any freehold interest in Stone Town Field, in the County of Stafford, are requested to meet at the Crown Inn, in Stone aforesaid, on Monday, the 28th day of August 1797, at 11 o'clock in the Forenoon, to consider the Propriety of applying to Parliament, in the next session, for an Act to divide the said Field."

A further meeting to hear a reading of the proposed Parliamentary Bill was held on November 6th, when "assent to or dissent from" was to be declared. Then on November 10th 1797[3] a "petition of several Persons, whose names are thereunto subscribed, was presented to the House and read: Setting forth, That there are, within two Certain Open Fields, in the Parish of Stone, in the County of Stafford, called *Stone Field* and the *Sandpits*, several Pieces or Parcels of Land, the property of the Petitioners and others, and also several Baulks and Waste Lands, which, in their present State, are incapable of any considerable improvement, but, if the same were divided, and specific Shares allotted to the several Owners thereof, and Persons interested therein, according to the respective Rights and Interests, the same might be enclosed and considerably improved."

The Bill was duly presented by May 1798,[4] it being then stated that "the Parties concerned had given their Consent to the Bill; except the Owners of 40 acres 2 Roods and 14 Perches of Land, who refused to sign the Bill; and that the whole Property interested in the Inclosure consists of 360 acres 3 Roods and 13 Perches, or thereabouts; and that no Person appears to oppose the Bill."

It is clear that those in favour of inclosure were the larger owners; those who had refused their consent were the small owners who had nothing to gain and much to lose from the inclosure of the open fields. "The lord of the manor", wrote the Hammonds,[5] "was given a certain quantity of land in lieu of his surface rights, and that compact allotment was infinitely more valuable than the rights so compensated. Similarly the tithe owner stood to gain with increased rents. The larger farmer's interests were in inclosure, which gave him a wider field for his capital and enterprise. The other classes stood to lose . . . the small farmer found himself deprived of the use of the fallow and stubble pasture, which had been almost as indispensable as the land he cultivated. 'Strip the small farms of the benefit of the commons', wrote one observer, 'and they are all at one stroke levelled to the ground.'"

This view was confirmed by the terms of the *Stone Award*, which received the Royal Assent on June 21st 1798. *John Jervis*, as owner of land, was given 10 plots totalling 110 acres, and a further 6 acres in lieu of tithes; *William Jervis* received 42 acres; *Thomas Swinnerton, as Lord of the Manor of Kibblestone*, received 2½ acres; the *Lord of the Manor of Stone* was now the *Marquis of Stafford*, who had acquired the extensive properties formerly belonging to the Crompton family as well as the manorial rights; under the award he received 23½ acres in lieu of hay tithes and as owner; *Ralph Wright* was allocated nearly 9 acres; the heirs of *Thomas Hatrell* 11½ acres; *William Boreham* 16 acres; the *"Curate of Stone"* almost 10 acres, his land being between the present Oulton Rd. and Old Rd., known thereafter as the *Parson's Field*, and bought between the two world wars for the housing development of Princes St., York St. and Queen's Square; *Thomas Dent* received three plots totalling 16 acres.

In the complete award and allocation at Stone, 28 owners received land; 19 of them received less than five acres each; the seven largest landowners together received 230 of the 360 acres involved. *All the householders in Stone, Meaford and Oulton* had held rights of common over these two fields, and in the award they were allotted 74 acres, "to be occupied from henceforth for ever in common by the Occupiers of Houses already erected and built, or hereafter to be erected and built, in the said Township of Stone, Meaford and Oulton, after the Rate and Stint of One Milch Cow for each House, and with no other Cattle, in lieu of all Right of Common watsoever." With minor adjustments to the Scheme of Management, the *Common Plot*, centred around the ancient *Motley Pits*, remains to this day for the benefit of the people, managed by a body of Trustees under the general control of the Charity Commissioners.

With the inclosing and fencing of these new plots, many new roads were constructed, under the Award, to give access. The *London to Liverpool* and the *Cheadle turnpike roads* already crossed the lands; a new road called *Meaford Farm Road* was made out of the rough track leading from Stone to that village. *Oulton Rd.* was made as a new road, branching out of the Cheadle turnpike, and continuing down what is now known as Nicholls Lane and on to Moddershall; also a road around the northern boundary of the Common Plot from Old Rd., and now part of the many minor roads known as the *Outlanes*. Nearer the town were the *Town-end Furlong* (now Margaret St.) and the *Middle Road* (now Whitebridge Lane), joining Meaford Road to the turnpike road which is now Newcastle Rd.

For Stone this inclosure meant not only a complete break with the older methods of cultivation. It meant also a change in the appearance of this part of Stone. Where there were two open fields before 1800, there were now 70 plots, each fenced with oak posts and rails on either side of a quickthorn hedge. With the exception of the Common Plot, these new plots were freehold property to be used for any purpose the owner might choose. Already inventions for the "new" agriculture were being shown:

> "Falcon Inn, Stone.
> A new invented Thrashing Machine will be exhibited at the above Inn on Thursday, the 12th inst. (October 1797) which, with the assistance of two men, will thrash as much in an hour as ten men can in the usual way."[6]

At the same time there were signs of industry developing in the town; the population was increasing (from 1500 to 3000 between 1801 and 1834)[7] and the need for more houses was becoming apparent. And so much of the inclosed land was used for housing, that by the end of the 19th century Stonefield had become the most heavily built-up area of the town.

But still, in the early 1800s the old continued to exist side by side with the new. A deed of 1803, referring to Lord Granville Leveson Gower's rights as Lord of the Manor of Stone lists "all those Tolls of Fairs and Markets, Courts Baron, Courts Leet and Pye Powder Courts thereunto belonging. . . ." The Court of Piepowder was derived from the French "pied poudreux", meaning "dusty foot", and was a court to deal with disputes arising at fairs, where many pedlars arrived on foot to carry on their trade. Lady Catherine Leveson Gower, "Lady of the Manor (of Stone) and owner of this Fair" issued this notice in about 1810:[8]

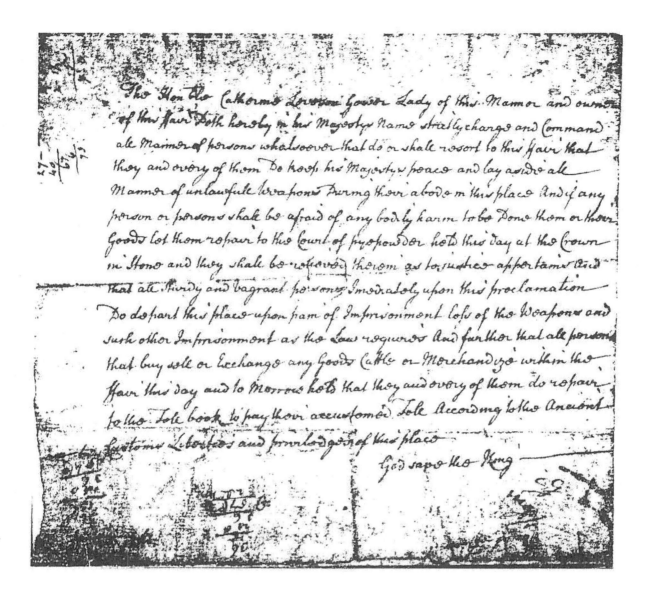

Proclamation of a Fair at Stone, c. 1810, by The Hon. Catherine Leveson
Gower, Lady of the Manor of Stone.
William Salt Library, 3/10/41.
reproduced by kind permission of the Trustees.

PLATE 14

"... all Manor of persons that do or shall resort to this Fair (shall) keep his Majesty's peace and lay aside all Manner of unlawful Weapons during their abode in this place. And if any person or persons shall be afraid of any bodily harm to be done them or their Goods let them repair to the *Court of Pyepowder* held this day at the Crown in Stone, and they shall be relieved therein as to justice appertains. And that all Sturdy and Vagrant persons Immediately upon this proclamation Do depart this place upon pain of Imprisonment, loss of Weapons, and such other Imprisonment as the Law requires. . . ."

That the town was increasing in size and in the variety of its trades was evident between the end of the 18th century and the first part of the 19th. In 1787 only three tradesmen were recorded. In 1818 *John Joule* was listed as a brewer.[9] In 1834 *James Lockett*[10] was brewing in High St., as were *Wenman Smith & Co.* In 1842 *Randall, George & Green* were also brewing in High St.

The Directory of 1835-6[12] had this to say of Stone: "The chief article of manufacture here is shoes; upon the Scotch Brook stream are flour and flint mills; malt is made in the town; and there is a small trade in timber and a boat-building yard." There were four *maltsters* in Market St.[13]—*Samuel Davison & Co., Thomas Hayes, John Nickisson* and *Thomas Tharme*, and there was also a *Henry Nickisson* in Elmhurst St. (formerly the Town-end Furlong and now Margaret St.) *John Joule & Son* were corn millers as well as brewers; *William Lathbury* was at Stone Mill, *Thomas and Richard Smith* were at "Bill's Mill" in Mill Lane,[14] *James Lucas* was a miller at Moddershall, and *James Wright* was at the *Windmill* in Lichfield Rd. *Coopering* was essential to the brewing trade,: engaged on this work in 1834 were Richard James in High St., Joseph Meredith in Stafford St., and James Nickisson in Chapel St.[15]

A number of the more individual craftsmen remained in 1828: William Hales, a *flint grinder* in Market St., Richard Hamalrack, a *chair maker* in (New) Castle St., Guy Vitta, *carver and gilder* in Elmhurst St.,[16] George Wright, a *locksmith* in Church St., there were two *nail makers* in Mill St., John Hudson and Richard Straw, while Robert Birch in Chapel St. was a *basket maker*. Two *coachmen*, Edward Lloyd and Joseph Ward, lived in Lichfield St., and another coachman, Thomas Sharratt, in Chapel St. In 1834 Edward Green and Thomas Sims were manufacturing *rope and twine* at the Limekiln, and Samuel Wilkinson was a *net maker* at "Newtown", which must have been the developing area of Stonefield. John Lawrence of Lichfield St. was a *brushmaker*, and so was Gabriel Ludford, the innkeeper of the aptly named 'Brushmakers' Arms' in Oulton.

In 1842 Daniel Timmis was a *linen and woollen draper* in the main street, as were William and John Nickisson, whose business was carried on in premises where the Midland Bank now stands. Old account books show that it had been carried on by at least five generations of the *Nickisson family*, and later by *Foden and Brandon*. *Straw hats* were popular in the early 19th century, and these were made in the town by Mary Beech of the Market Place, and by Sarah Shaw and Sarah Cartwright in Chapel St., while H. Wardle of High St. was a *straw bonnet maker*. It is not surprising that by 1851 the High St. was "of considerable length and has many well-stocked shops."

By 1818 William Dixon was no longer the only recorded shoe manufacturer, as he had been in 1787. *Charles Bromley* and *Joseph Bromley* were *manufacturing shoes* in the Market Place and in Market St., and *Thomas Warrilow* had established premises in the New (Lichfield) Road. Indeed, the 1821 directory[17] stated: "There is a large manufactory of shoes carried on, one of the most considerable in the kingdom, principally for the London market."

Each year new manufactories of boots and shoes sprang up: John Lycett and Joseph Lawton in the New Road, Thomas Warrilow in Oulton Rd., John Woollaston in Market St., John Bloor in Oulton Rd., James Goodall in Church St., and John Goodwin in Market St. In 1834 there were sixteen boot and shoe making "shops", nine of which were wholesale manufacturers. Supporting this trade were George Thorpe of Church St., a *last maker*, and John Aston and Charles Bromley, both with *tanneries* in Stafford St. A considerable number of the town's inhabitants were employed in the making of shoes, for which, in 1834, "this place is as important as Stafford, and the extensive manufacturers here also employ many of the cordwainers in the surrounding villages." This rapid growth of "industry", unchecked and unguided, created problems of health and sanitation for later generations to solve. Meanwhile the richer classes enjoyed their separate life, and in 1834 William White[18] recorded that "during the last 20 years many of the inhabitants have built handsome dwellings in the suburbs of the town, on the Lichfield, Newcastle and Longton Roads, and on the opposite side of the Trent in the pleasant village of Walton."

The self-sufficing villages soon ceased to exist: improvements in roads and the carriage of goods by canal meant that people now bought in the towns articles which their fathers and mothers had made for themselves.[19] The increased use of transport was of great importance to Stone, and coaches, which were now safer, quicker and more popular, ran to a fixed schedule through Stone.

COACHES FROM THE CROWN INN

The *Mail Coach* to *London*, daily at 7.30 a.m., to *Liverpool* daily at 3.30 p.m.

The *Mail Coach* to *Birmingham* daily at 7.30 a.m., to *Manchester* daily at 3.30 p.m.

The *Prince Cobourg* to *London* daily at 7 a.m., to *Liverpool* daily at 10.45 a.m.

The *Prince Cobourg* to *London* daily except Sunday at 9.30 p.m., to *Manchester* daily except Monday at 2 p.m.

The *Eclipse* to *Birmingham* daily at 1.30 p.m., to *Manchester* daily at 12.15 p.m.

COACHES FROM THE UNICORN INN

The *Prince Cobourg* to *London* daily at 9.30 p.m., to *Manchester* daily at 2 p.m.

COACHES FROM THE BELL AND BEAR INN

The *Expedition* to *London* daily at 6 a.m., to *Liverpool* daily at 10 a.m.

The *Umpire* to *London* daily at 9 p.m., to *Liverpool* daily at 11 a.m.

The *Bang Up* to *Birmingham* daily at 3 p.m., to *Liverpool* daily at 11.30 a.m.

The *Regulator* to *Birmingham*, every Tuesday, Thursday & Saturday at 2.30 p.m., to *Liverpool* on the same days at 12 noon.

For the carriage of goods by road, *Ashmole's waggons* left the Falcon Inn for Birmingham on Mondays at 12 noon, Wednesdays at 8 p.m. and Saturdays at 12 noon; for Manchester every Tuesday, Thursday and Saturday at 8 p.m. The *Post Office* was still at the Crown Inn; letters arrived and were sent by the mail coaches, and there was a bye-mail to Cheadle every day.

In 1834, the peak year of the stage-coach, no fewer than 38 coaches passed through Stone every day,[20] many of them with fascinating names: Erin-go-Bragh, Express, Paul Pry, Hark Forward, Red Rover, Aurora, Rocket, Traveller and Pottery Lark, in addition to the ones listed above. The coaches also used the Blue Bell[21] and Falcon inns.[22] All the coaching inns had extensive stabling, reaching far back from the main street. In comparison with the present number of inns, the list for 1834 was very long, and contained many which have now gone. This was the 1834 list:

Antelope, High St. (now Ferrie's Flower shop)
Bell and Bear, High St. (now G. M. York, furnishers)
Black Horse, High St. (now the Super-market)
Blue Bell Inn, High St. (now Town Hall/Cinema)
Brewers' Arms, High St. (now Bradley's (Chester) Ltd.)
Crown Inn, High St.
Falcon, High St.
Fountain, High St. (now Barclay's Bank)
Hand & Trumpet, New(castle) St. (now part of St. Dominic's Convent grounds)
King's Arms, High St. (next to Jackson's butchers & recently the premises of George Mason Ltd.)
Lamb, Walton (now demolished and since replaced twice)
Red Lion, High St.
Rising Sun, Limekiln (still in Newcastle Rd., and still with access to the canal near the Limekiln Lock)
Robin Hood, Church St.
Roe Buck, Stafford St. (now Stafford St. car park)
Royal Oak, Stafford St. (backing to the gasholder and now demolished)
Star, Stafford St. (had stabling for the narrow-boat horses; this stabling has recently been demolished)
Unicorn, High St. (now shop development for George Mason Ltd. and others)
Vine, Oulton Rd.
Wheat Sheaf, High St. (now H.S. York, electrician)
White Lion, High St. (now closed for re-development)

Beer Houses
Boat, Newcastle St.
Brown Jug, Lichfield St.
Samuel Fenton, Mill St.
Gardeners' Arms, High St.
Jolly Crafts, Church St.
George Marlow, Newtown.
Union, Newcastle St.

All these beer houses have ceased to exist as such.

On the canal, even by 1818, there were sixteen different firms of carriers, ready to carry goods from Stone to all parts of the country, and the *Canal Company's Wharfinger*, responsible for controlling all this traffic, was Francis Smith. He would have seen the first experimental steam-boat on the canal in 1828, making its way from London to Liverpool and back. The expense of propelling such a boat was stated to be "only one-third of that required when horses are employed; and when an additional boat is towed, the expense will not be one-eighth,"[23] but the idea was not taken up until the days of the petrol engine.

During the period when the town's population doubled, the number of people in the whole Stone Parish increased from 2843 to 7806. The parish was divided into four quarters, for each of which a churchwarden was appointed, as well as an overseer. The parish as a whole cared for the poor, at a cost of £6,000 per annum, and the parish workhouse in Stone was described in 1834 as "a large brick edifice, having more the appearance of a gentleman's villa than a house of industry, having a handsome front, a small lawn shaded with trees and about 3 acres of land."[24]

The old parish officers remained: *Job Astbury* of Oulton Rd., was the constable, and his brother *John* was the *town-crier and pounder*. But this simple form of control was being re-inforced by the institution, in 1829, of a magistrates' court which sat every fortnight, with *Ralph Adderley* of Barlaston Hall, and *William Bewley Meeke* of the Brooms as magistrates, and William Dutton, a Stone solicitor, as clerk.[25]

Stone was now becoming more than a small market town; it was, in the early part of the 19th century, laying the foundations of industrial development. Its position in the Trent valley, blessed with means of communication which were capable of both improvement and change, made it possible for Stone to escape the fate which befell so many of the communities which had had their origin in the shelter of a religious establishment, and had declined after the dissolution. Stone survived and grew, and the seal of confidence in its future was set by the building of a savings' bank in Pump Square (now Granville Sq.) by the *Pirehill and Meaford Savings Bank*, which had started in 1818. In November 1850 its deposits amounted to £30,749. The sum of £24,396 belonged to 777 individual depositors; £4,318 to Twelve Friendly Societies, and £463 to eleven Charitable Institutions.[27]

NOTES AND REFERENCES

1. These details are from Arthur Young: Six Months' Tour through the North of England, 1770, vol. III., pp. 258f.

2. Stone Weekly News, 19 November 1909.

3. Journal of the House of Commons, 10 November 1797.

4. ibid. 23 May 1798.

5. J. L. & Barbara Hammond: The Village Labourer, 1760–1832.

6. Staffordshire Advertiser, 7 October 1797.

7. William White: History, Gazeteer & Directory of Staffordshire, 1834, pp. 669–671.

8. See plate 14, and note how this old notice was scribbled on before coming into the safe keeping of the William Salt Library.

9. Staffordshire General & Commercial Directory of 1818.

10. William White: History, Gazeteer & Directory of Staffordshire, 1834.

11. Pigot & Co.'s Royal National and Commercial Directory, 1842.

12. Pigot & Co.'s National Commercial Directory, 1835–6.

13. The lower (and newer) part of High St.

14. Later known as Stubbs' Mill.

15. Later North St., now part of Station Rd.

16. Now Margaret St.

17. G. A. Cooke: Topographical and Statistical description of the County of Stafford, London, c. 1821.

18. History, Gazeteer & Directory of Staffordshire, 1834.

19. G. M. Trevelyan: Social History of England, p. 374.

20. William White: History, Gazeteer & Directory of Staffordshire, 1851.

21. Now the Town Hall/Cinema.

22. S. A. H. Burne: The Coaching Age in Staffordshire (N.S. Field Club Trans. vol. lvi (1921–22) p. 56).

23. Staffordshire Advertiser, 20 September 1828 and 11 October 1828.

24. William White: op. cit., 1834, pp. 669–671.

25. Staffordshire Advertiser, 17 January 1829.

26. Since demolished and its place taken by Stone Post Office.

27. William White: op. cit. 1851.

CHAPTER 12

SCHOOLS AND SPORTS

After the re-siting of the Grammar School on the edge of the Parish church-yard, there were one or two vain efforts to improve the school, but after 1814 it reached rock-bottom. The Rev. Joseph Smith, a curate at Stone, received the salary of £13. 6s. 8d. as nominal head, at the very time that he was usher of the Grammar School at Stafford, where he was reported to be thoroughly lazy. In 1824 the Senior Bursar of Trinity College had to visit *Stone* for first-hand information,[1] and discovered that Smith had not lived in the town for a year, had never taught in the school, and that "no one in Stone ever remembers a Grammar School taught there." With Alleyne's school failing, at this stage, to live up to its founder's expectations, other families interested themselves in education.

The Jervis family (of Darlaston) were responsible for the provision of a school near Stone on the south side of Newcastle Rd. In 1744 William Jervis of Newcastle, by his will, gave £100[2] to be used for such charitable purposes as his nephew, John Jervis of Darlaston, and his heirs, should think fit. By his will, dated 12th January 1774, John decided that the interest of this sum, a £5 yearly rent charge, should be used for the instruction of poor children in the parish of Stone, and he himself added a further rent charge of similar amount. The Charity Commissioners' Report of 1825[3] stated that the Jervis's school was known as the *Froghole School*. In 1801 when the land on which the school stood was enclosed, Mr. Jervis took down the school and removed the materials to Darlaston, with the intention of rebuilding it. But Mr. Jervis died in 1802, before this could be done, and the money was then used for the maintenance of a school in Darlaston, kept by a Mrs. Emery, who, for the income of the endowments and an additional sum of £10, the voluntary gift of Lady St. Vincent, taught 31 girls to "read and to work". In 1841 the prescribed instruction included reading, writing and accounts, and the principles of religion,[4] and William White, in 1851, recorded that the school was then in the Mill House, which was surrounded by water, and some-times flooded for three or four days together. This would be the mill on the Trent, behind Darlaston Inn, the site being now between the two river bridges.

Private schools were also available to those who could afford: Mr. and Mrs. Quinclet moved their school for ladies from Walton to Oulton Hall in 1799,[5] and their terms were:

"Board, including English grammatically, and all sorts of Needlwork, per annum	£14 14s. od.
Entrance	£1 1s. od.
Music, per Quarter	£1 1s. od.
Entrance	£1 1s. od.
French, grammatically, per Quarter	£1 15s. od.
Entrance	10s. 6d.

Dancing, per Quarter	15s. od.
Entrance	10s. 6d.
Drawing, per Quarter	15s. od.
Entrance	10s. 6d.
Writing and Arithmetic, per Quarter	6s. od.
Entrance	2s. 6d.
Washing, per Quarter	10s. od.

French is constantly spoken in the Family, and the utmost care is taken of the Health and Morals of the Young Ladies.

By 1818 *William and Charles Boreham* (Field Place), *Thomas Ash* (Abbey Court or St.), *Hannah Matthews* (Church St.) and *Margaret Oxley* were all running their own "academies". While the standard of education given in these establishments was reasonably good, there was, both locally and nationally, a need for some form of basic education. This was first met, in Stone, in 1832, when the National Society, supported by subscriptions, opened the *National School*, built on a site adjoining Abbey St., on the lower part of what is now the old St. Michael's school playground. By 1851 this school had 200 pupils. In the belief that this was an exclusive Church of England school, the British and Foreign School Society, which claimed a universality which welcomed children of all beliefs, held a meeting at the Crown on February 11th 1834, supported by William Ridgway, John Joule, and others, and a subscription list was opened. A building was erected in 1842 in the back "Radfords", beyond the present Christ Church parish room. In urging the building of this school, John Joule had admitted that "whereas he had formerly thought that the education of the working classes, when carried beyond a certain extent, was injurious, he now believed that education led men to think; instructed them generally, though correctly; the greatest danger was in their not thinking at all." Thus were started the town's two elementary schools, firstly St. Michael's and then Christ Church.

This zeal for education among a rapidly rising population was accompanied by a great upsurge of religious fervour. During the winter of 1833–34 the curate-in-charge of the Parish Church found it necessary to run Sunday Evening Lectures, which were, in effect, a duplication of the normal service. To give support to his efforts, the Bishop "travelled to Stone on six or seven tempestuous Sunday evenings". To a large extent these extra services were a direct result of selling the pews in the parish church as freehold property. In 1838 there were, within two miles of the parish church, 466 families, representing 2092 people, belonging to the Church of England, without a pew in the church. The only free sittings were on benches in the aisles, sufficient to seat 162 worshippers.

With little or no hope of "freeing" the pews, talks began between Viscount St. Vincent of Meaford Hall, the Rev. Charles Simeon who had expressed a desire to endow a church in Stone, and the Rev. Francis Kitchen, to establish a church to serve not only the growing northern area of Stone with a population now of 1561, but also the Darlaston, Meaford, Tittensor, Oulton and Moddershall parts of the old Stone Parish. The first site selected for the new church was at the top of Radford St., but the railway company already had rights to this land, and a piece of land nearer the town was given by Earl Granville. The foundation stone was laid on June 28th 1838, the coronation day of Queen Victoria, by Viscountess St. Vincent, and the church was consecrated by the Lord Bishop on April 23rd 1840. An endowment of £1000 was given on behalf of the Rev. Charles Simeon, and the Rev. Francis Kitchen was appointed first vicar of Christ Church.

Meanwhile the struggle to save Alleyne's School went on. The so-called headmaster held on to his salary, though he did not reside in Stone between 1823 and 1840. After a visit in 1840 a new Bursar of Trinity College, Mr. Francis Martin, found that only the parish had a key to the upper room, and decided that it was useless "to do anything with the building so long as any portion of it is claimed (whether with justice or not) by the Parish, and also till a new master resident in the place is elected instead of Mr. Smith".[6] The College then faced a predicament, for the College lawyer stated that in accordance with the foundation they were bound to maintain a school building, to pay a master's salary, and to continue the school as a Grammar School.

The passing of the Grammar School Act of 1840 allowed the introduction of subjects other than those laid down in the foundation.[7] This was some relief to the College, but it also encouraged the *Rector of Stone*, the Rev. *Gibson Lucas*, to try to merge Alleyne's school with the Parish National School. On March 5th 1841, the Rector wrote:

"The school room is tumbling down—indeed some of it has fallen—which renders it untenable", and six weeks later: ". . . each scholar pays as much or more than he does elsewhere, and learns no more than he would in the National School. . . . It is the Bishop's wish, and seems to be that of the parish, that it could be incorporated in the National School."[8] .

Almost at the same time the Rev. Francis Kitchen, vicar of the newly established Christ Church, whose schools were not built until 1842, also wrote, on May 3rd 1841, to Trinity College:

"No doubt you are aware that your Schoolhouse is now a heap of ruins, and that this parish is now divided into two ecclesiastical districts worked as two distinct parishes . . .   I therefore hope in the renovation of your School house you will take into consideration the position of Christ Church district in which are the majority of the children of the town without School houses."[9]

The College agreed to increase the stipend of the master to £100 per annum and to open negotiations for the revival of the school. The Rector continued to press: "I cannot at present see any advantage a grammar school is to be unless it can, by some means, be connected with the National School. . . . There is already a very good school here[10] at which the Classics are taught for 4 guineas a year." By 1842 the windows in the old school were smashed or boarded up, and the Rev. Gibson Lucas was removing desks. The townspeople of Stone with real concern for education must have been relieved when the College bought, for £248, a site for a new grammar school in Station Rd. The Rev. Joseph Smith, who had caused so much trouble, was "induced to resign";[11] Trinity College then took the unfortunate step of appointing to the headship *Mr. Charles Boreham*, who, as his father had done before him, conducted the school at Field Place. The appointment was made with the advice and concurrence of the Rev. Gibson Lucas, and the College soon had reason to regret it.

While this had been going on, other new developments had been taking place in the town. The Nonconformist interest in Stone awoke to new life towards the end of the 18th century with the visits of *Captain Jonathan Scott*, who held services in Pump Square. Eventually a chapel was built in North St. in 1786[12], probably from money chiefly provided by Scott, who certainly owned the manse, which he left in his will to *Francis Joule*, then the mainstay of the Stone Chapel.[13] Many active ministers served the chapel after Scott's time, among them the Rev. Thomas Newnes, whose son was Sir George Newnes, founder of the publishing firm of that name. It was during the pastorate of the Rev. Thomas Adams (1853-1860) that the music in the North St. Chapel was supplied by an orchestra of violins, flutes, cello and bass fiddle. Mr. Robert Morris, a watchmaker, played the bass fiddle, and one of the violinists was Mr. W. B. Woolley, postmaster of Stone and senior deacon of the church.

Wesleyan Methodism had a great struggle in its early days, with a chapel in Abbey St. in 1821, then, about 1850, services over Bromley's shoe factory in Lichfield St.; but the lack of a proper chapel caused an abandonment of effort until later in the century.

Stone was also very concerned at this period by the introduction of railways, especially when the line through Norton Bridge and Stafford was opened. Even at the very busiest time of coach travel, there was a "Railway Coach" which left the Swan Hotel at 10.30 every morning for the Potteries, via Stone, returning in the afternoons to meet the 5 o'clock trains at Stafford. A second coach, called simply the "Railway" began a similar run from the Saracen's Head in Hanley, through Stoke, Longton and Stone to Stafford, and back again, to connect with the trains at Stafford. The fact that it was now possible to go by train from Stafford or Norton Bridge to London, Birmingham, Gloucester, Liverpool or Manchester, led to a rapid falling-off in the number of stage-coaches; the mail coaches were taken off the roads in 1841.

Stone's trade suffered severely from the disappearance of the coaches, for the town was a long way from the nearest railway. For many years Stone passed through periods of alternate hope and despair. In 1839 a proposal to establish a *gas-company* in Stone had included powers "to lay mains through lands to any railway station that may be made within the township". This was intended for a station on a proposed Stone to Rugby line and a Manchester to Stone line via the Potteries. Large towns, such as Birmingham, were against it in the hope of getting a monopoly of trade; Lord Harrowby opposed it because it would pass through his Sandon estate. Even so, the Stone and Rugby Extension Railway Bill, supported

THE "BLACK HORSE" INN, HIGH STREET, DEMOLISHED IN 1954.

THATCHED COTTAGE REMAINING IN CHURCH STREET IN 1841.
based on a drawing by J.C.Buckler, 22nd June 1841 (Brit.Mus.Add.Mss.36387.f.236)

PLATE 15

by "upwards of 600 influential persons" got through the Committee stage in Parliament, but no further owing to the dissolution of Parliament.

Stone was again by-passed when a railway was constructed from Stafford to Rugby, and it was not until July 1846 that the royal assent was given for the construction of the North Staffordshire Railway. This comprised a line from Macclesfield to Stoke, *Stone* and Colwich, at which place it would join the Stafford-Rugby railway; and it included branch lines from Harecastle (Kidsgrove) to Crewe, and from Stone to Norton Bridge. Work began immediately on the northern end of the line, and on February 11th 1847 the cutting of the first turf for the Norton Bridge branch line took place in a field adjoining the Gosdells, now the Stone Golf Course. *Viscount St. Vincent* cut the turf with a new spade and wheeled it away in an oak barrow specially made for the occasion. A great procession had moved from Stone to the scene of the ceremony, and there were between five and six thousand people present. The poor, the aged and the children were all given meals during the day, and in the evening there was a dinner at the Crown. It was Mr. Bromley, shoe manufacturer, who replied to the toast: "Prosperity and wealth to the town of Stone", and he said that

"he had been a resident of the town for many years, and was connected with the staple trade of the place. He remembered when Stone was one of the most thriving little towns in the county of Stafford. He was alluding to the palmy days of coaching. . . . These coaches were a great advantage to it, inasmuch as they brought persons from the densely populated towns of Yorkshire and Lancashire, where the manufactures of Stone were so much required; they did so in preference to the rival manufacturing town of Stafford, seven miles further on. When these coaches were stopped *(c. 1840)* by the introduction of railways, it caused a great set-back to the trade of the town, from the effects of which they were only then *(1847)* recovering. . . . He hoped that from the opening of the railway, they would be once more raised to the position they occupied some years ago."

By the end of March 1848 the line from Stoke to Norton Bridge was finished. The first trains came through Stone on April 3rd, goods only being dealt with for the first fortnight. A traveller on *the first passenger journey* has left his impression:

". . . the whistle now notifies that we are near a station. Rush goes the train past Field House, over a girder bridge thrown across the canal, and we halt at a temporary station at the entrance to the *town of Stone*, where the arrival of *the first train* is hailed with satisfaction by a very numerous assemblage of admiring spectators.

"The stoppage for a few minutes to take in passengers enables us to step out, and see what progress the railway workers are making in this neighbourhood. We find that the main line is only complete as far as the junction with the Norton Bridge branch upon which we have entered. Preparations are being made to erect a handsome station near the point of junction. Like most stations on the main line, the building will be in the Elizabethan style. There will also be cheese and corn warehouses, sheds, shunts for cattle, coal yards, and every appurtenance required by the commerce of the extensive agricultural district of which Stone is the chief mart. The temporary station is erected close to the ornamental stone and girder bridge, with handsome balustrades, which crosses the Newcastle Rd. It is gained by two flights of steps. The platform commands a view of the town and neighbourhood.

"The bell rings, seats are resumed, and again we proceed on our journey."

At first four trains each way on weekdays, and two on Sundays, were run between Stone and Norton Bridge, passengers changing there to join the Manchester and Birmingham trains. The week following the *opening of the railway* was a holiday week, and to provide facilities for the people of the Potteries, "special third-class trains were announced to run from Stoke to Trentham and Stone, the fare to Trentham and back to be threepence, and *to Stone and back again, sixpence.*" The success of these railway "excursions" was immediate, and, as Whitsuntide drew near the newspapers reported that "the influx of visitors by excursion trains to Stone was so great at Easter that the victuallers were fairly eaten out of house and home. To be forewarned is to be forearmed, and ampler provision will prevent another sacking of the Stone larders."

By May 1849 the line to Colwich was completed, and Stone was once more a route centre, and able to overcome the temporary eclipse which the railways had at first brought. As an agricultural centre Stone had never ceased to flourish, and in 1834 *fortnightly cattle markets* had been established. On the opening day, August 26th "about 1100 sheep were penned, which met a ready sale. Fat cows and bullocks were in great numbers, but owing to the host of customers were not equal to the demands. At Mrs. Tharme's (the Unicorn) upwards of 40 gentlemen dined, consisting of dealers from Manchester, Birmingham, Shropshire and Macclesfield, and neighbouring farmers and graziers." For these markets the sheep were penned on each side of the High St., and in Pump Square; pigs in the Market Square; while cattle occupied Radford St. and Newcastle St. There were several well-known cattle dealers in the district, notably Shelley and Bridgwood of Aston.

In the town the streets were indifferently surfaced, and at night unlighted. The safe journeying of people along these dark streets depended largely upon the link-boys who, with their torches of tow and pitch, would guide them to their destination. The mission completed, the boys would "snuff" their torches in the extinguisher provided at the side of the door, as can still be seen outside Cumberland House. Public order and behaviour left much to be desired, especially at night. In 1840 Edward Sutton, known as the "old tramp shoemaker" was found, at 4 a.m., seriously injured in the "Antelope" entry, leading from High St. to Crown St. and the canal; he died later. He had left the "Antelope" at twenty past one in the morning, and the inquest jury made this report on

"... the state of the town of Stone from want of an effective police: public houses are open to a late hour, some of them, it is feared, nearly all night; consequently, drunken men are continually rolling about the streets all hours in the night, and frequently on the Sabbath day, cursing and swearing, to the great grief and annoyance of the peaceable inhabitants, hence every species of mischief."

Improvements were on the way, however. The *Stone Gas Light and Coke Company* set up a small gas-making plant in Crown St. in 1850, supplying gas at from 6s. 8d. to 8s. 4d. per 1000 cubic feet. In 1851 there were ten street lamps, which were paid for by subscription.[14]

Changes were now taking place in the amusements of the people. By 1800 cock-fighting and bull-baiting had lost some of their appeal, but had not completely gone. A new form of sport was introduced in 1823, when *Stone Races* were held on October 8th and 9th; a Gold Cup and Plate were entered for, as well as Sweepstakes and matches. The innovation was a success for "the number of people from all quarters exceeded calculation and it is confidently expected that ultimately Stone Races will not appear the most insignificant in the sporting world." These race meetings were held in the Station Meadow, a site now occupied by the factory of Messrs. Taylor, Tunnicliff & Co.[15]

In 1823 the old brutal sports had continued:

"The ancient but anti-christian practice of bull-baiting has been in full vigour this week. The amusement of tormenting a domestic animal began early on Sunday, and many persons were annoyed and alarmed on their return from the morning service at the Church by the bull being driven into the town preparatory to Monday. The poor bull did not at first make good play, and his horns being so set that he could not toss the dog, it was calculated that by Wednesday they would be able to worry him to death, but he improved and made good use of his feet, so as to kill several of his assailants, but having his nose and face lacerated in a most pitiable manner. . . . We rather expect that the races at Stone, which we hear have been excellent and well attended, will another year supersede bull-baiting."

And in 1824: "this being the second year only of these races, the sport, the concourse of people, and the vehicles of all descriptions, exceeded the most sanguine expectation; and it is pleasing to observe that this truly English amusement has completely superseded the barbarous custom of bull-baiting in Stone."

In the year 1828 the races were not held, and the old sports were back for the last time in Stone: "Stone Wakes this week were attended by a great number of holiday folks, who enjoyed the rustic amusements provided for them with zest. We are sorry that the races were discontinued, and bull-baiting, fighting and other sports substituted, in which the jolly Potters excelled all their competitors, especially those of Stone." The next year the race meetings were resumed and continued for many years, except in 1832 when a terrible outbreak of *cholera* ravaged the country, "annual fairs and race-meetings were cancelled, and a day of national prayer and fasting was ordered."

Many other forms of Wakes' sports and amusements were popular at this time. There was roll and treacle eating: rolls coated with treacle were hung up in the Market Square; with hand tied behind their backs, men tried to bite at the rolls while their treacle covered faces were dusted with feathers. There were also: climbing a greasy pole for a leg of mutton; racing in sacks from Pump Square to Stafford St.; "splashing the brook", or racing up the Scotch brook as far as Stubbs' mill,[16] wheel-barrow races down the High St.; "goose-jingling" or trying to catch, when blindfolded, a man with a bell, the prize for catching him being a goose. All these added to the fun of the Wakes, in which Willie Joule, Frank Turner, John Bowyer and William Emery were the prime movers. The

STONE RACES, 1838.

THE HON. W. B. BARING, M. P. } STEWARDS.
W. B. MEEKE, ESQ.,

Will take place on Tuesday and Wednesday, the 2nd and 3rd, days of October

TUESDAY, OCTOBER THE 2nd.
A SWEEPSTAKES

OF FIVE SOVEREIGNS each, with TWENTY SOVEREIGNS added for Horses that have never won 100 sovs. at any one time. Three years old to carry 7st. 12lbs.; four years old 8st.; five years old 9st. 7lbs.; six years old, and aged, 9st. 12lbs. Half-bred Horses allowed 7lbs. a winner once within the year to carry 3lbs.; twice 5lbs.; thrice 7lbs. extra. Heats thrice round and a distance.

SAME DAY.
THE HACK STAKES

OF THREE SOVEREIGNS each, with TWENTY SOVEREIGNS added from the Fund, for Horses not thorough bred, bonafide the Property of Subscribers residing within fifteen miles of Stone, that have never started, or been in the hands of a Trainer previous to the day of entry. To be ridden by the Owners, or Persons not being regular Jockies; three years old to carry 9st. 7lbs.; four years old 10st. 5lbs. five years old 10st. 12lbs.; six years old and aged, 11st. 2lbs. Heats twice round and a distance.

PRESENT SUBSCRIBERS,
J. R. MARSH, ESQ. | F. PRATT, ESQ. | Mr. W. MEESON.

WEDNESDAY, OCTOBER THE 3rd,
THE PUBLICANS' PURSE

OF THREE SOVEREIGNS each for any Horse, with a Sum not exceeding FIFTY SOVEREIGNS added from the Fund; weights and conditions same as for the five sovereign Stake the first day, the winner of which to carry 5lbs. extra. Heats thrice round and a distance.

SAME DAY.
The Hurdle Race

OF THREE SOVEREIGNS each, with FIFTEEN SOVEREIGNS added from the Fund, for Horses not thorough bred, and bona fide the Property of Subscribers residing within twenty Miles of Stone; three years old to carry 9st. 7lbs.; four years old 10st. 2lbs. six years old and aged 11st. 7lbs.; Mares and Geldings allowed 3lbs. A winner of a Hurdle Race in the present year, to carry 5lbs. extra, twice 7lbs. and thrice 10lbs. extra. Heats twice round and a distance, with four leaps in each Heat. If more than four Subscribers, the second horse to receive 3 sov. out of the Stakes.

☞ TO START EACH DAY AT TWELVE O'CLOCK.

No Money will be added to any of the Stakes if walked over for.—No Horse will be allowed to start unless he stands at the House of a Subscriber

The Horses to be entered with proper Certificates and Qualifications at the Crown Inn, on Monday Evening, the 1st of October, between the hours of Seven and Nine o'Clock. All entries and nominations to be delivered, sealed to the Clerk of the Course and to be declared for their respective Races, at a quarter past Nine. The colour of the Rider to be then declared. Any Rider changing his colour to pay 2s. which will be strictly enforced. The owner of each Horse to pay 10s. on the day of entry, for the use of Scales and Weights, and each winner to pay 15s. to the Clerk of the Course.

The instructions for clearing the Course will be strictly enforced. All persons are requested to retire behind the ropes on the bell ringing for saddling, to prevent accidents.

All disputes to be referred to the Stewards, or to whom they may appoint. Their decision to be final.

All Dogs found upon on the Course will be destroyed, and any person wilfully trespassing across the Fences will be prosecuted.

No person will be allowed to erect Booth, Shed, Stall, &c., until he has agreed with the Clerk, and paid his Subscription.

MR. LLOYD, Clerk of the Course.

Ordinaries at the CROWN INN, each day at the conclusion of the Races. (Tickets including Dinner and Desert 5s.)

E. BARKER, PRINTER, MARKET-PLACE, STONE.

PLATE 16

streets were lined with stalls, selling toffee and gingerbread, shooting galleries, swing-boats and merry-go-rounds, the latter being pushed around by the man in charge.[17]

Foot-racing had also become popular, and Bill Brown, the "Pet of the town" was a great runner in the hurdle and handicap racing in the Crown Meadow. In 1840 this notice was issued:

"STONE STEEPLE CHASE
open to all the world,
Will take place on Wednesday, October 7th. 1840 at
Half-past Eleven precisely, and under the following conditions:
Two Sovereigns for the Winner
Thirty Shillings for the Second,
Ten Shillings for the Third,
Ten Shillings to be spent after the Chase.

To be run for by men of all countries, starting at the Grand Stand of Stone Race Course, then crossing the Canal, to proceed between Posts or Flags (to show the line of Ground) over the New and Old River Trent, to the Turnpike Gate of the Filleybrooks or Hamilton Lane, to touch it and return the same way back to the Grand Stand, at which who first arrives will be the winner."

Daniel Dawson, Hon. Sec."

In the same year of 1840 a group of enthusiastic townspeople introduced half-yearly *cheese fairs* on the third Tuesdays in October and May. For the first of these fairs waggons and carts were ranged on each side of High St. and more than 100 tons of cheese changed hands, and in 1841 the amount had risen to 200 tons. The honorary secretary for these fairs was *John Nickisson*, who was elected a member of the Royal Agricultural Society of England.

The year 1842 saw the riots connected with the *Chartist movement*. Although Stone was near to the Potteries, where there were serious disturbances aimed at securing better conditions for workers in the new industries, and also near to Stafford where special assizes were held, the town did not have to go beyond the stage of taking precautions. The local magistrates, Viscount St. Vincent and W. Bewley Taylor, enrolled over 700 special constables, drilled by the military forces (34th Infantry) stationed in the town. This notice was displayed throughout the district:

"NOTICE AND CAUTION
We, the undersigned Magistrates of the County of Stafford, in conformity with Her Majesty's Proclamation, deem it our duty thus publicly to make known, that all assemblages of persons having a manifest tendency to endanger public peace, and to excite the fears of Her Majesty's peaceable subjects, are illegal . . .
We further order and direct all publicans, keepers of beer houses and dram shops, to close their houses at ten o'clock every night, and not allow the same to be opened before six o'clock on the following morning, or permit any malt, liquor or spirits to be drunk therein between those hours of the night and morning, under the pains and penalties of the statute in such cases made and provided.
GOD SAVE THE QUEEN.
ST. VINCENT
W. BEWLEY TAYLOR.
Stone, August 18, 1842."

Patrols of special constables paraded in the streets every night, and the press reported that "there was a strict adherence to order from all classes."

In 1851 a police station of the county constabulary was established in Newcastle St. with Thomas Woolaston as police inspector.

The billeting of troops in the town was a regular occurrence, Stone having the accommodation in its numerous inns. The officers' mess was at the Crown, which had now become known as hotel rather than inn, and the townspeople had the pleasure of gathering outside the Crown to hear the playing of the regimental bands. Other regular visitors were the Irish labourers, chiefly from Galway, who came over for seasonal work, especially at harvest-time. They lodged chiefly in Newcastle St. or Stafford St., or slept in barns all week and came into the town at week-ends. They often quarrelled among themselves and brawled with the people of Stone, and they were not particular about weapons, the sickle often being used. There was plenty of gleaning done, too, by the poorer families, but the gradual introduction of machinery ended both the gleaning and the need for the Irish labour.

At the beginning of the 19th century two men were living near Stone who were to achieve distinction in their separate ways. *Henry Fourdrinier* was born in London on February 11th 1766, his father being a paper-maker and wholesale stationer. He and his brother Sealey worked for many years on paper-making machinery, the first patent being taken out in 1801. By 1807 they had perfected their machine for making continuous paper, of any size. Large sums had been spent on the invention, but although the new method was widely adopted, the law of patents was then so defective that the brothers were virtually ruined. In 1814 the Emperor Alexander of Russia, while visiting England, entered into an agreement with the Fourdriniers for the use of two machines in return for an annual payment of £700. The machines were erected in Russia under the supervision of Henry Fourdrinier's son, but never a penny of the agreed sum was paid. At the age of 72 Henry went with his daughter to St. Petersburg, to plead personally with the Emperor Nicholas, but with no success.

The British Parliament was asked to consider compensation for the losses sustained, and on May 8th 1840, a sum of £7,000 was voted to the Fourdriniers. Many people thought this inadequate, and a few years later firms in the paper trade, including "The Times", organised a subscription which purchased annuities for Henry Fourdrinier, the sole surviving patentee, and his two daughters. Some time before this, he had come to live at *Burston* Hall, where he had celebrated his golden wedding. His wife died the following year and was buried in the Parish churchyard. Henry later moved to a small home at Mavesyn Ridware, near Rugeley, where he lived humbly and happily until his death on September 3rd 1854 in his 89th year. He too was buried in the vault in the southern part of the churchyard, near Lichfield St., where the monument over the vault was left in position when the churchyard was recently levelled. *Henry Fourdrinier's* name occurs in 1839 in the first of the minute-books of the "Hanley Felons" Association", an organisation of business people to protect themselves against felons, and he was the founder of the paper-making firm which became Brittain's Paper Mills.

At this same period, at Oulton, in the building now better known as Oulton Abbey, was the establishment of *the Bakewells*. *Thomas Bakewell* had been born at Cheadle in 1761, where he later became manager of a Tape Mill. While holding this position he studied the subject of insanity under two of his uncles, and in 1808 he bought from the Jervis family the property known as Spring Vale near Tittensor. Here he established an asylum for the insane which was very successful. He was also a poet of some ability, among his works being "The Moorland Bard, or Poetical Recollections of a Weaver in the Moorlands of Staffordshire."

By his third wife, Sarah Glover of Hanford, he had eleven children. When he died on September 6th 1835, at the age of 79, his eldest son, *Samuel Glover Bakewell* (born at Spring Vale in 1811) was carrying on the work, having become a Doctor of Medicine at Edinburgh University in 1833.

In 1840 the Spring Vale property was sold to the Duke of Sutherland for £11,000, and the asylum removed to Oulton:

"*Oulton Retreat*, a large and well-conducted private Lunatic Asylum belonging to Mrs. Sarah Bakewell, and under the superintendence of Samuel Glover Bakewell, M.D. . . . This retreat for patients of the higher and middle classes, was formerly called Oulton House, and is a large and handsome mansion with park-like lawn of considerable extent, commanding extensive and pleasant prospects."

"The Metropolitan Commissioners in Lunacy have spoken in high praise of this asylum, and of Dr. Bakewell's successful mode of treatment."[19]

The asylum was later moved to Church Stretton, and the Oulton property passed to the Benedictine Nuns, becoming St. Mary's Abbey. The Bakewell vault and monument are in the parish churchyard, not far from the south-west corner of St. Michael's Church.

NOTES AND REFERENCES

 1. Trinity College Muniments: Stone School, Box 33(I.b).
 2. Stone Parish Church Benefactions Boards.
 3. Charity Commissioners, 13th Report, 1825, pp. 338–9.
 4. Digest of the Reports of the Commissioners of Inquiry into Charities, 1841, Staffordshire, p. 75.
 5. Staffordshire Advertiser: the files of this newspaper have been used extensively for this period.
 6. Trinity College Muniments: Stone School, Box 33 (I.b).
 7. S. J. Curtis: History of Education in England, 1948, p. 61.
 8. Trinity College Muniments: Stone School, Box 33 (III.b).
 9. Trinity College Muniments: Stone School, Box 33 (I.c).
10. The Borehams' school at Field Place.
11. Trinity College Muniments: Stone School, Box 33 (I.c).
12. Site now occupied by part of St. Mary's Home.
13. A. G. Matthews: The Congregational Churches of Staffordshire, 1924, p. 133.
14. William White: History, Gazeteer & Directory of Staffordshire, 1851.
15. Named on the Ordnance Survey Maps as the Racecourse Works.
16. The Scotch brook was then open between Crown St. and High St., where it now flows under the Stafford St. car park.
17. Stone Weekly News, 8 October 1909.
18. See Pigot & Co.'s National & Commercial Directory, 1842; Stone: Links with the Past, p. 40; Dictionary of National Biography; and Staffordshire Advertiser, 8 February 1936.
19. William White: History, Gazeteer & Directory of Staffordshire, 1851.

CHAPTER 13

CATHOLIC REVIVAL

Throughout the reign of Elizabeth I the Heveningham family of Aston had struggled to keep alive the Catholic faith, and their effort continued when a descendant of the family, Bridget, married *Sir James Simeon*, and when Margaret, the daughter of this marriage, married *Humphrey Weld*.

In 1789[1] *Aston Hall* was described as a large H-shaped building, standing in its own extensive grounds and surrounded by a moat. In these grounds, under the cover of the trees, Sir James built a large mausoleum for the interment of himself and his family. It is not believed that later members of the Weld family actually lived at Aston, but the earlier members always kept a resident priest there. About 1769 Ralph Sneyd was living at Aston, and when he left the house began to fall into decay, being only occasionally inhabited by a Catholic priest who held services for the villagers in the chapel of the hall.

Towards 1800 Mr. Weld decided to sell most of his Aston estate to *Earl St. Vincent*, who is said to have paid for it with the prize money he had collected at sea. A large portion of the Hall was pulled down, and Mr. Weld set aside the remainder of the house, some fields and an orchard for the endowment of a Catholic mission. A group of *Bridgettine nuns* came in 1809 to Aston and tried unsuccessfully to maintain an establishment there. In 1818 came a body of *Franciscans* who were at first very successful and added considerably to the house, but their effort faded after five or six years, and after 1831 there was only a secular priest left at Aston.

On September 28th 1840 Dr. Wiseman invited *Father Dominic* to take charge of the mission at Aston Hall. This famous man (who was beatified in 1963) was the son of a poor labourer in Italy, and in his early youth was himself a shepherd boy and farm labourer. Born on August 4th 1793, he took his name from the fact that his birthday was the feast day of St. Dominic, and he joined the order of Passionists in 1814, later becoming a lecturer in theology at Rome, and Rector of the Convent of St. Angelo di Tramonta at Lucca. He longed constantly to work in England, and the invitation to Aston was just his chance. Father Dominic arrived at Aston on February 17th 1842, and opened a religious house to which he gave the name of St. Michael's Retreat; in this he was helped by an endowment of about £80 from Mr. Weld. From the outset Father Dominic did not confine his missionary work to Aston, but included *Stone* also, though the town was largely Protestant. His first sermon was preached from a cart in a field which now forms part of the gardens of St. Dominic's convent. Then the assembly room of the "Crown" was hired on Sundays, and fittings supplied by Mr. James Beech, then the town's most prominent Catholic, transformed it into a chapel. There were few immediate results of his efforts, even though he came two or three times a week to Stone, but Father Dominic seemed to sense that a revival would eventually come. When a man lamented the destruction of the town's Augustinian Priory, Father

Dominic answered:

"Never mind! You will live to see, though I shall not, another Convent and another Church, not at the bottom but at the top of the town!"

Many were the insults Father Dominic had to endure during the early years; often he was pursued with abuse and ridicule. Once a party of youths began to pelt him with mud and stones. Thereupon Father Dominic knelt down, and picking up the stones as they fell about him, kissed them devoutly. The boys, astonished and ashamed, withdrew and never molested him again. Being unable, by now, to endure the thought of services being held in a hotel, Mr. Beech set aside a room in his own home, *Elmhurst House*, in what is now Margaret St. but which has been known as Elmhurst St. At the same time Mr. Beech gave land across the road for a small permanent chapel, to be built largely at his expense. This chapel was designed by *Augustus Pugin*, dedicated to St. Anne, and was opened and blessed by Father Dominic on April 22nd 1844. This chapel continued to serve the Catholic community in Stone until 1853, when Mr. Beech gave the land and the chapel to Mother Margaret. It still stands as a monument to the combined labours of Father Dominic and Margaret Hallahan, but it is now within the grounds of the convent.

The peak of Father Dominic's career was in 1845 when he received into the Church of Rome the Rev. J. H. Newman, a former Church of England minister and one of the leaders of the Oxford movement. Newman, who later became a Cardinal in the Roman Church, had written to a number of his friends:

"Littlemore, October 8th 1845. I am this night expecting Father Dominic, the Passionist. . . . He is a simple, holy man, and withal gifted with remarkable powers. He does not know of my intention, but I mean to ask of him admission into the Fold of Christ."

The year 1847 saw the founding of the church of St. Michael at Aston, the first stone being laid by Dr. Walsh, and Cardinal Wiseman preached the sermon. The church was opened in 1849. During these years the Passionists had found themselves in great demand in the Stone and Aston districts, for many of the poor Irish, leaving their famine stricken country, had begged their way here, only to be laid low with fever. The wards of the workhouse would not take half of the sufferers; every hovel and barn had its sick and dying, and local people were afraid to go near. The Passionists did, and those who were not themselves stricken, worked day and night to bring comfort to the suffering, helping them until they recovered, or died fortified by the rites of the Church.

Father Dominic died at Reading on July 27th 1849, and his body was brought to Stone *to rest in the chapel of St. Anne*. Large crowds filed through the chapel to pay their last respects, amongst them many of the Irish harvest labourers. When the funeral cortege left for Aston, almost all Stone turned out to pay homage to the man who had once met with ridicule. When the Passionists left Aston in 1854

St. Anne's Chapel, designed by Augustus Welby Pugin. The Chapel was opened and blessed by Father Dominic in 1844.

St. Dominic's Convent founded by Mother Margaret Hallahan in 1853.

Plate 17

Father Dominic's remains were removed and now rest at St. Anne's Retreat at Sutton, near St. Helens.

With the death of Father Dominic, the state of the Passionist community at Aston was precarious. The church, opened in 1849, was not finished; by 1854 the community had broken up, and parts of the old hall were pulled down. Meanwhile, in *Stone*, Mr. Beech had become acquainted with the work being done in Longton by Mother Margaret Hallahan, and in 1851 he offered to her the little chapel of St. Anne, and an acre and a half of land on which to build a convent.[2]

This remarkable woman was born in London in 1802, of respectable Irish parents, who had become sadly reduced, and by the time she was nine years of age both her parents had died. A lady in Moorfields took an interest in her, and sent her to school; she stayed for three years, and this was the only schooling she had. She later went to work with a family in Bruges, and remained in Belgium for fifteen years; while there she took the vows of the third order of St. Dominic. Then in 1842, in her fortieth year, she asked to return to England to assist Dr. Ullathorne, who was then a parish priest at Coventry. In a very short time she had organised a school of 150 children; when she had arrived at Coventry the number of communicants was 50, but in a few years the number was increased to 550. At Coventry, too, she began a conventual establishment of which the original number was four.

When Dr. Ullathorne was made Bishop of the western district, Mother Margaret and her sisters went with him to Clifton, where she founded a convent. Later she set up orphanages at St. Marychurch near Torquay, and at Bow in the east end of London. In 1850 Dr. Ullathorne was made Bishop of Birmingham, and she came back to the Midlands, and first of all to Longton. After four years the small Longton convent moved to Stoke, and Mother Margaret came to Stone to accept Mr. Beech's invitation.

In *1853* she was able to buy a piece of land and some cottages adjoining the land already given to her, and the sisters moved in. Their strange dress soon evoked comment, and it seemed that they would have to face a campaign of persecution. But the sisters were not deterred from visiting the homes of the sick and the poor, taking with them a feeling of truth and sincerity, and soon the name of *Mother Margaret Hallahan* became a household word, and the sisters were an accepted part of the town's life. On the 4th of August 1853 the foundation stone of the present *St. Dominic's Church* was laid by Dr. Ullathorne. The architect of the new building was *Joseph Hansom*, who also designed Birmingham Town Hall, but who is probably better known for his invention of the hansom cab. Mother Margaret's belief was that "God would provide", and the size and beauty of this church are an example of her faith. The church was blessed and opened by Dr. Ullathorne on May 3rd. 1854, with seating for 500 people. At the east end of the south aisle is the altar of St. Winifrede, and the altar reredos shows St. Chad baptising Wulfad and Rufin, the Stone martyrs, and their death at the hand of their father Wulfhere.

Mother Margaret and her sisters continued to visit the sick and poor; another cottage was taken and, despite their limited resources, a few aged and sick women were housed there. This was the early beginning of St. Mary's Home. She found time, too, for educational work. As early as March 1857 two sisters came from the Potteries for the 'inside' of the week to teach in the little school she had started in St. Anne's Chapel. Then, having barely completed a church far in excess of the immediate requirements of the Catholic population, she began to look for a site for a larger school. A position bordering on Newcastle St. was acquired and a girls' school erected. It remained under the direct control of the sisters until 1877, when it became a mixed school. Her charity and goodness never flagged and when work was scarce, or winter's grip was upon them, the poor always found the convent door open to offer help. One extremely severe winter, distress was great among the canal boat people, with their boats ice-bound. So regular was her visiting in their troubles that they, in spite of their tough natures, came to regard her as a ministering angel.

As the members of her community increased in numbers and their sphere of work extended, the convent required to be enlarged. More land was acquired, but a path crossed this land to the "Hand and Trumpet" in Newcastle St. An unknown benefactor had already left Mother Margaret £2,000 to commence a real hospital, and when, in 1860, the "Hand and Trumpet" unexpectedly came up for auction, the community purchased the inn, two cottages and an acre of land for £1500.[3] Wonders of accommodation were wrought within these properties, and more patients were accepted. Once she exclaimed: "I wish we could build a big place and take in everybody". It was in 1871, three years after her death, that the wish came nearer to reality, when St. Mary's Home was transferred to Elmhurst House, opposite the church, and once the home of their original benefactor, James Beech. Through all these labours Mother Margaret bore a heavy load of personal suffering. From her seventeenth year she had suffered from a spinal disease. She had not complained, but even *her* endurance had to yield in November 1867. She lingered on, in extreme pain, for six months, giving her community final instructions. She died on the night of May 11th. 1868, and was buried in the church at Stone which she had built. The chapter-house of the convent treasures the statue of the Blessed Virgin which Mother Margaret brought from Belgium, and also a portion of the hair shirt worn by Sir Thomas More.

Mother Margaret was the direct agent in founding five convents,[4] two schools, four churches and several orphanages and hospitals. When she came to Stone there were about 50 Roman Catholics; in 1868 there were 1300. Bishop Ullathorne, who, besides serving 38 years as Bishop of Birmingham, had in his early days worked as a chaplain among convicts transported to Australia and had done much to end this cruel practice, died in 1889. He lies in an altar tomb in the Stone Church. Both Cardinal Newman and Cardinal Wiseman were visitors to the convent, and when the latter came to Stone in 1884 the rifle band played at the convent while his Eminence dined.

This remarkable revival of the Roman Catholic faith in Stone had taken place in little more than twenty years, and a similar growth was apparent in the Church of England. *John Ford* became vicar of Christ Church in 1853, and served the district for 30 years. An infant school and a master's house were added in 1856 to the schools in the Radfords; in 1870 further schools were built in the Stonefield area to serve the ever-growing population there. And he himself added a paddock to the vicarage grounds, and land for the extension of the churchyard in 1868. However, John Ford's most memorable work was, perhaps, what he did for the outlying parts of the parish. The National School built in Oulton, soon after 1860, served for many years as church and school, and a similar institution was established at Tittensor. But this did not satisfy John Ford, who was determined that these growing villages should have *real churches*. A church in *Oulton* was begun in 1875, and consecrated on July 17th 1878. At *Tittensor* the foundation stone of a church was laid on June 18th 1880 by the Duchess of Sutherland, and the ceremony was unique because of the presence of the Prince of Wales (later Edward VII) who was then staying at Trentham Hall. *Meaford and Darlaston* now remained. Lady Forester built schools there in 1880, to serve as church also, and John Ford took the first service there on·July 3rd 1881, to be followed by weekly services from the mother church in Stone. When John Ford retired in 1882, he was given, by parishioners and friends, a purse containing 400 sovereigns.

Apart from new buildings, all around were signs of the new ways, rapidly replacing the old. The newly introduced fortnightly cattle markets were succeeding, but the old fairs were declining:

In 1851 it was recorded:
"The old fairs have been discontinued, except that on August 5th for sheep, &c.,"

and in 1865:

"Stone Fair, which was formerly of considerable dimensions, has gradually declined until last Saturday the stock consisted of two cows."[5]

The importance of the Wakes was also waning, and in 1874 the opinion was expressed that "the festival now serves no good purpose whatsoever, and would, in common with similar events throughout the country, be more honoured in the breach than in the observance. On Sunday there was a large influx of visitors, chiefly from the Potteries, of a class who found their principal amusement in drinking, and its accompaniment of quarrelling, swearing and fighting."[6]

The *town-crier* remained in Stone until well into the 20th century. In 1851 *John Lawton* held the post; in 1860 *William Higginson* took the job over from his father, and continued until 1904, when his own son succeeded him.[7]

Changes were taking place in the trade of the town, too, and not without some resistance. In 1851[8] it was stated that

"the shoe manufacture, which has long been the great staple trade of the town, has for some time been in a flourishing state, and a new suburb has begun to be built near the new (Christ)

Church. Stone is as famous for shoes as Stafford, and its extensive manufactures employ many of the cordwainers in the surrounding parishes."

The list of shoe-makers in 1851 included 27 names, 13 of them engaged in the wholesale trade. But very soon after this list was published, difficulties began to develop as mechanisation replaced the hand processes. A machine was introduced at *Musson's factory*, and two girls were set to operate it. Immediately the work people were roused against this machinery, which, it was believed, would cause widespread unemployment. Angry crowds surrounded the girls as they left work, men and women joining in, so that police protection became necessary. The trouble ceased when a number of the ringleaders were sent to prison.

When *Bostocks* introduced machinery the opposition was so intense that the machines were transferred to Leicester. Then violence in an uglier form broke out when the firm planned to make men's boots in Stone; local workers refused to attend the factory, and Irish workers were brought from Liverpool. These new men were subjected to all kinds of insult and violence, and eventually an open rupture resulted in serious injuries being inflicted. The Rector of Stone, the Rev. Eldred Woodland, volunteered to act as mediator, and he succeeded in getting work resumed at the factory. In an address to the local shoemakers, he reminded them of the importance of science and machinery in raising their standard of living, and of the folly of resisting progress:

"My advice to you is, if there is anything good in this dreaded machinery, or this new system, and you are bent upon driving them away, depend upon it—so surely as you succeed, so surely will a new trade spring up in places where it is impossible to put into use such means as are in your hands, and the market will be won from you by those very means which were once within your reach, and which alone would have enabled you to keep it."

Similar troubles occurred early in 1858, when all but three of the manufacturers were "blocked" by the refusal of their hands to work, with serious effects on the town's trade.[9] A similar strike in Stafford's shoe trade at this time lasted five months, but *Stone's difficulties* were happily settled by mutual concessions after a little more than a fortnight.[10] The next dispute in the trade was the sub-division of labour, an inevitable result of the tendency to larger factories and increased mechanisation. On Wednesday evening, April 29th 1863, in the yard of the "Black Horse" Inn, a meeting of five or six hundred shoemakers unanimously carried resolutions condemning the factory system "as commenced by Mr. Thomas Bostock of Stone, and threatened strike action if Mr. Bostock refused to give up making stitch-work on the premises."[11] When Mr. Bostock stood firm, the strike began, endorsed by members of the Amalgamated Society of Cordwainers by 1152 votes to 126.[12] After a struggle lasting 15 weeks, the strike ended on August 22nd in "an unconditional surrender to the proposals of Messrs. Bostock."[13]

The new methods in the manufacturing trades led to a need to watch closely the working conditions, especially as they affected women and children. This was not easy, as this report of 1873 showed:

"There are in the town four 'factories' (employing over 50 hands each) and eight or ten 'workshops' of considerable size and easily discoverable, though employing less than 50 hands. But I found that large numbers of persons were employed in the trade besides those in the above 12 or 15 establishments; and I obtained from the principal manufacturer in the town a list of no less than 116 houses to which work was taken from his warehouse. It was impossible to tell without inspection how many of these places of work contained female or juvenile workers, and were therefore 'shops'. I spent, accordingly, two days in visiting some of them, knocking from house to house, and occupying nearly as much time in finding one or two as would have sufficed to inspect a factory employing 500 hands. I did not visit them all; for as the occupiers of all the factories and large workshops send out work in the same way, there are probably 400 or 500 houses in the town wherein boots are made. . . . Subsequently, in consequence of complaints, I visited a few houses in which children were said to be employed, and sent them to school; but considering that these families are continually moving from cottage to cottage . . . no-one but a local man, intimately acquainted with the town and its inhabitants could hope to enforce the law. Everyone on the spot knows this to be the case; and the gentleman who gave me the list referred to laughed sadly when I told him for what purpose I wanted it."[14]

In 1874 it was estimated that 1600 people in Stone were engaged in the shoe trade, a considerable portion of whom were females.[15]

The enthusiasm for education continued unabated. In 1852 the *Mechanics' Library and Literary Society* had started in St. Michael's National School, not only consolidating the library established in 1848 by the Rev. Francis Kitchen, but introducing lectures and classes on all subjects at fees within reach of everyone.

In 1843 Trinity College announced the opening of a new Grammar School building[16] in Station Rd., with Mr. Charles Boreham as headmaster, and immediately under this announcement came one from Mr. Boreham to the effect that his own Field House school would still continue "under his own immediate superintendence". A storm of protests followed these announcements. Only one person seemed satisfied, the Rev. Gibson Lucas, who reported in June 1844 that Charles Boreham had given up Field Place to his brother, and was devoting his whole attention to Alleyne's, and in November of that same year he reported the school as "satisfactory as to management and efficiency, though not full".[17] The Rev. Gibson Lucas was either ignorant of the state of affairs, or wilfully misleading. Fortunately, Mr. J. P. Norris, M.A., who lived in Stafford and was attached to the Education Office in London, sent an independent report on the school to Trinity College. On July 19th 1856, Mr. Norris wrote to the Bursar:

"Today I found the school still a lumber-room, occupied by barrels, harness, old furniture, bags of seed &c., among which the school apparatus and books were lying about. In one of the school desks, the hinges of which were broken, was lying a fowling-piece, with shot and caps scattered about. . . . I have reason to believe that the school has been more or less in this state ever since my last visit." Mr. Norris suggested an inspection, "in the hope that Mr. Boreham would best consider his own interests by resigning or carrying out his long formed intention of emigrating."[18]

THE NATIONAL SCHOOL (ST. MICHAEL'S) IN LICHFIELD STREET, OPENED IN 1858 A.D.

ALLEYNE'S GRAMMAR SCHOOL AT OULTON CROSS IN 1889.

PLATE 18.

The inspection took place on September 29th 1857, and the report was devastating; it included this remark: "Mr. Boreham farms 10 acres, of which two acres are part of the school estate . . . and it is evident that he takes much interest in his farm, and but little in his school." In 1858 Mr. Boreham, who, incidentally was a nephew of the Rev. Joseph Smith, was persuaded to resign; Mr. G. Wade took over the headship, and by 1862 it was clear that he had restored the good name of Alleyne's.

William White's directory of 1851 gave evidence that the elementary schools in the town were playing their part efficiently: the Parish Church school had 200 children, Christ Church school some 300, even though at this time parents had to pay 2d. or 4d. each week for the education, and attendance was not yet compulsory. By 1856 the National (St. Michael's) School was inadequate, and when the land between the school and Lichfield St. was conveyed to the Trustees, a new school with a teacher's residence was built facing Lichfield St. The school was opened in 1858, and is still in use.

After the ending of the stage-coaches and the mail-coaches, the Post Office left the Crown for premises in Pump Square. Here *Mrs. Sarah Key* was *postmistress*, and Jesse Davis the clerk. In 1842 the mail came by train to Stafford, and then by *mail cart* to Stone:

"Letters from all parts (except Cheadle) arrive every morning at seven, and are despatched every evening at nine. Letters from Cheadle arrive (by mail gig) every night at half-past eight, and are despatched every morning at half-past seven."[19]

By 1851 there were considerable improvements, with *Mr. Jesse Davis* now *postmaster*. Letters were sent to all parts "at 1½ afternoon and 10 night, and the letter-box closed at 1¼ and 9½ p.m."[20]

The mail-cart bringing the letters from Stafford to Stone in the early hours of the morning caused a complaint to be sent to the Post Office in 1883 about the driver's "too frequent blowing of the postman's horn to give warning of approach."

Another feature of life in Stone at this time was the revival of the *Volunteer Movement*, which had ceased after the end of the Napoleonic wars. In 1858 an attempt was made on the life of Napoleon III and it was known that the would-be assassins had come from London; in consequence French officers demanded to be led against "the land that sheltered monsters". The British response was to authorise Lords Lieutenant of the counties to "nominate proper persons to be officers, subject to the Queen's approval, of *volunteer rifle corps*."[21] In September *1860 Stone* subscribed £200 towards the formation of a *rifle corps*, and 80 volunteers had given in their names.[22] Stone became the 40th Company, attached to the 1st Staffordshire Battalion. Soon the company had its own band, and rifle-shooting contests (at the Downsbanks) became an annual event. A report in 1877 said:

"Captain Bromley is fortunate in possessing a staff of zealous and soldier-like non-commissioned officers, who have ably seconded his exertions, which have resulted in the present high state of efficiency, of which every member of the corps may be justly proud."[23]

The *fire-fighting* in the town also depended on voluntary efforts. The first fire-engine was probably the *parish engine, dated 1787*, kept in the church porch. Then there were *Evans' Parish Brigade* and the *Volunteer Brigade*, who later joined forces. They had a "Defiance" engine, and later the "Sutherland" manual engine, purchased in 1882 by subscription. The Birmingham Insurance Company also kept an engine in a shed near the site of what is now St. Michael's Hall. In 1886, when Mr. (later Colonel) Harding was in charge of the town's volunteer brigade, a new engine (horse-drawn, of course) was bought with the proceeds of a bazaar, and christened "*Edith Mabel*" in honour of Mr. Harding's youngest daughter.[24]

In the middle of the 19th century, large numbers of the people were dependent upon the many *Friendly Societies* for benefits in time of sickness and financial help with funerals. Long before National Insurance, the small weekly contributions of all the members helped to tide the less fortunate over times of difficulty. The town had the Modern Druids,[25] the Female Druids,[26] the Loyal and Independent Order of Gardeners[27] and the Stone Fair Friendly Society. At a meeting of this last-named society on July 19th 1841, *Mr. Daniel*, who had been surgeon to the Society for 23 years, said that

"Stone Fair Club was the noblest institution of the kind which Stone had ever produced ... and that during the last ten years it had paid to its sick and superannuated members, and for members' funerals, nearly four thousand pounds."[28]

One of the events eagerly looked forward to was the Ladies' Club Festival. This was really a display of fashions "and when crinolines were worn, two of the women took up the greater part of the street. After a feast at the 'Blue Bell' there was dancing as long as the band could play."

There was, of course, always the less pleasant aspect of life. The practice of sending small boys into chimneys to clean them was made illegal in 1842, yet in October 1854

"a master sweep of this town (Stone) was charged before the magistrates, at the instance of the Association for Suppression of the Employment of Children in Chimney-Sweeping, with employing a boy to sweep chimneys, and was fined £5 with costs ... the inspector employed by the association is still on the alert, and it would be well if parties wishing to escape the penalties would direct their servants to insist on the use of the machine."

In 1854 Britain had entered the *Crimean War*. People in Stone contributed generously to the national fund for relieving hardships for nurses and troops in the winter of 1854. Recruiting sergeants were busy in the town, young men being almost "pressed" into service in return for the Queen's shilling; the militia went abroad, the Stone men going to Corfu, and news of the war was eagerly awaited outside the shop of Mr. Gundry, printer and newsagent. The fort of Sebastopol fell in September 1855. Unofficially the news of its fall reached Stone at about nine o'clock on the evening of September 10th, and large crowds awaited the arrival of the London mail at 4 a.m. the following day. Within half an hour of its arrival the union jack was flying from the church tower and the bells were ringing.[29]

When the Treaty of Paris was signed in the following year there was a procession which included *Crimean heroes on horseback;* tea for the children and the poor, and a firework display; and at the end of the week "public joy was manifested by a dance in the open street which was kept up with great spirit until a late hour."[30]

A little more than a week after this Stone had a different kind of excitement, the occasion of the public hanging at Stafford of *Dr. Palmer, the Rugeley poisoner.* During the night thousands of people tramped through Stone from the Potteries and even from places further north, and there were "overladen spring carts, omnibuses, many with four horses, and all descriptions of vehicles."[31] It was said that almost every man in Stone walked to Stafford to see his execution.

In September of that year a *Stone centenarian* died at the age of 103. This was *John Hodson*, who up to the year before his death

"was to be seen daily driving the cows to milk through the town, and with the exception of his hearing, he had the perfect use of all his faculties to the end. He had been a member of the Stone Fair Club, and his family proudly kept the light blue frock coat which he wore on 60 consecutive "days" at the Stone Fair Club."[32]

The horse-races had now ceased, but by 1845 cricket was being played:

"Stone Royal Victoria *Cricket Club:* the members of this club (which has but recently been formed) held their first meeting on Good Friday. The playing of this noble and manly game was enjoyed for several hours, after which the members adjourned to the "Unicorn" inn, and did ample justice to the excellent catering of Miss Tharme."[33]

Prize-fighting was still popular, but discouraged:

"Considerable excitement among a certain class was evinced . . . by a fight for a sovereign-a-side taking place on Tittensor Common. Some 290 or 300 persons were watching the contestants, *Joseph Myatt* and *Thomas Taboner*, shoemakers, *of Stone*. The fight continued three parts of an hour when the cry: "Look out, the bobbies are coming" resounded, and immediately the crowd scattered. Police officers Goodall and Sheldon gave chase and captured the pugilists, who were brought up on Tuesday, bound to keep the peace for six months, and ordered to pay costs."[34]

After 1879 the North Staffordshire Hunt *Steeplechases* were for a number of years held at Stone, and the cricket continued, on the Redhill ground in 1874[35] and on the old race-course in 1880.

Another source of interest was the annual show of the *Stone Horticultural Society*, of which Mr. James Lewis was secretary for many years. The first show was held on July 27th 1869 in a tent outside the Pirehill and Meaford Savings Bank in Pump Square. The first show of the *Staffordshire Agricultural Society* was held in Stone in 1844, in the Boat Yard. In 1853 the show was at Meaford, when "lambs were shown with long tails tufted at the end like the caudal appendage of the king of beasts." The 1876 show was at Mr. Thomas Bowers' farm, and that of 1884 at Mr. Weaver's farm. In *1894 the Jubilee Show* was held in Stone and the town excelled itself with decorations and illuminations, and concerts were given each evening by the *Stone Military Band*. In 1906 when the show was again held in Stone the entries and the quality were up to average, and the weather was glorious, but receipts were down and a loss was sustained.[36] It was 1938 before the show paid its next, and last, visit to Stone, using farm-land in and near Whitemill Lane, Walton, which was later used for war-time housing.

Finally, there were efforts made by religious bodies other than the Roman Catholics and Christ Church to meet the needs of the growing population. The Parish Church made the first of many attempts to remedy the evils arising from the sale of pews in 1758. Reminding his parishioners at vestry meetings that no provision had been made for worshippers who did not own pews, except for "a few uncomfortable benches thrust into the middle aisle", the *Rev. Eldred Woodland* stated that during the 100 years since rebuilding, pews were possessed by inheritance or purchase, by owners all over the country, and even abroad. Many were also owned by people living in the "new district" of Christ Church, and who were attending that church. Quite a number of these owners demanded rents for the use of their pews in the parish church and there were cases of "pews locked up by the owners because they were not taken at a rent."[37] The evil was indeed acute when one owner instituted County Court proceedings for non-payment of the rent of a pew. But the problem was too big to be solved in a single operation, and in 1878 improvements were limited to the substitution of chairs for the benches, and re-positioning the pulpit and reading desk.[38] In the following year a new rectory was built in Lichfield Rd. to take the place of the building now known as the Priory.

When the Rev. J. P. Bake came to the Congregational Chapel in North St. in 1868, he found serious defects in the roof and extensive repairs needed elsewhere in the building. It was considered better to rebuild than to repair. *Mr. Thomas Bostock* gave a piece of land, valued at £300, at the junction of Longton Rd. and Granville Terrace, and the foundation stone of the new church was laid on September 6th, 1870 by Mr. John Crossley of Halifax. This new building, completed during 1871, soon became a landmark in the town, with its spire rising to a height of 80 feet. It had accommodation for 700 worshippers, besides vestries and classrooms.[39] The first services were held on November 13th 1871, and a new organ was installed and used for the first time in May 1876.

Methodism also overcame its problem of accommodation too. A revival had come in 1879, when the *Rev. Edward Smith* preached on Saturday evenings by the old town pump. A room was then secured in Edward St., and by September of 1879 there was a "congregation of nearly 200 persons, a Church of 70 members, and a Sunday school attended by more than 100 children". Efforts were renewed to find a permanent home, and on September 9th 1879 the foundation stones were laid of a new *Methodist Chapel* on a site in the Avenue, planned to seat 300 persons. The first services were held in June 1880, and the Rev. Edward Smith, recalling this achievement, said: "In July 1879 the way was opened and Methodism was planted in Stone".

NOTES AND REFERENCES

1. The Topographer, vol. I., June 1789, p. 118.
2. See a) Rev. P. D. Corbishley: Margaret Hallahan (London, 1958, Catholic Truth Society).
   b) Sister Mary Reginald Capes: Stone and its History (Rosary Magazine).
   c) Staffordshire Advertiser, 16 May 1868.
3. Staffordshire Advertiser, 21 July 1860.
4. Stoke, Torquay, Clifton and Bow are affiliated to Stone.
5. Staffordshire Advertiser, 12 August 1865.
6. ibid. 10 October 1874.
7. Stone Weekly News, 19 August 1904.
8. William White: History, Gazeteer & Directory of Staffordshire, 1851.
9. Staffordshire Advertiser, 13 February 1858.
10. ibid. 27 February 1858.
11. ibid. 2 May 1863.
12. ibid. 11 July 1863.
13. ibid. 22 August 1863.
14. Report of the Inspector of Factories, Staffordshire Advertiser, 19 July 1873.
15. J. C. Tildesley & others: Staffordshire and Warwickshire.
16. Now part of the workshops of Messrs. Banks & Bennett, builders &c.
17. Trinity College Muniments: Stone School: Box 33 (I.c).
18. ibid. Box 33 (III.c).
19. Pigot and Co's National and Commercial Directory, 1842.
20. William White: op. cit. 1851.
21. Theodore Martin: Life of the Prince Consort, vol. iv.
22. Staffordshire Advertiser, 15 September 1860.
23. ibid. 1 December 1877.
24. Stone Guardian, 24 February 1962 and 3 March 1962.
25. Staffordshire Advertiser, 25 May 1844.
26. ibid. 29 August 1840.
27. ibid. 24 July 1841.
28. ibid. 31 July 1841.
29. ibid. 15 September 1855.
30. ibid. 7 June 1856.
31. ibid. 14 June 1856.
32. ibid. 27 September 1856.
33. ibid. 29 March 1845.
34. ibid. 11 April 1863.
35. Stone Weekly News, 19 April 1907.
36. Staffordshire Chronicle, 10 April 1938.
37. Staffordshire Advertiser, 13 May 1865.
38. ibid. 21 December 1878.
39. ibid. 10 September 1870.

THE OLD HALL AT DARLASTON

THE OLD HALL AT MEAFORD, BEFORE LADY FORESTER'S NEW PORTION WAS BUILT.
THE PART IN WHICH JOHN JERVIS, EARL ST. VINCENT, WAS BORN IN 1735, IS ON THE RIGHT.

PLATE 19.

CHAPTER 14

JOINT EFFORTS TO BENEFIT STONE

The history of the *Jervis family* in the Stone area has always been complicated by the fact that there were two branches of the family living at Meaford and at Darlaston in the 17th century. Both these villages had had a hall[1] for many years before this, the lands of each being divided only by the river Trent. The Jervis family had come from Chatcull, and towards the end of the 17th century John Jervis was living at Meaford, while his brother William was at Darlaston, having bought that estate from James Collier in 1655. In the course of time both the *Meaford and Darlaston estates* passed into the hands of *William Jervis*, the elder brother of Earl St. Vincent, and later, when William died without children, to the Earl himself.[2]

When the Earl died in 1823, also without children, the Earldom was ended, but *the Viscountcy* passed to his nephew, Edward Ricketts, the son of his sister Mary. Edward changed his surname to Jervis by deed-poll, and became the *2nd Viscount St. Vincent*. Edward, this 2nd Viscount, had *first married* Mary Cassandra, daughter of the 10th Lord Saye and Sele, but this marriage was dissolved by Act of Parliament in 1798, although the descendants of this marriage have continued the line of Viscounts to the present, 7th Viscount.

Even before he succeeded to the Viscountcy, Edward Ricketts had contracted a *second marriage* with Mary Anne, daughter of Thomas Parker of Park Hall, and from this marriage there were two children: *Mary Anne*, born in 1812, who was to play a large part in the development of the town of Stone, and *Edward Swynfen*, born in 1815, who, by royal licence in 1861, assumed the additional title of Parker, and thus became the ancestor of the Parker-Jervis family.

In the year 1840 *Mary Anne Jervis* married an Indian named *Dyce Sombre*[3] of Sirdhana in Bengal. Under a treaty made in 1803 with the Duke of Wellington, the land of Sirdhana passed to the East India Company, but the Begum retained control over her personal possessions, and shortly before her death in 1836 she made Dyce Sombre her heir. Within a year of acquiring his wealthy inheritance, Dyce Sombre had left Sirdhana; he arrived in London in 1838 to make a marriage with Mary Anne which was to prove disastrous. In 1841 Dyce Sombre was elected M.P. for Sudbury in Suffolk, a borough with a bad reputation for bribery at elections, and the following year he was deprived of his seat in Parliament for "gross, systematic and extensive bribery", and the borough lost its right to elect a Member. In 1843 a commission declared him to be of unsound mind from October 27th 1842, and his wife was allowed an annuity of £4,000 until his death in 1851. Lady Cardigan, in her "Recollections" says that Dyce Sombre had tried to suffocate his wife.

His will, made in 1849, was contested by Mary Anne, and she became involved in legal processes with the East India Company which lasted for five years. The final hearing lasted 19 days, and *judgement was given in the widow's favour*. As a result Mary Anne acquired jewels and immense personal property, reputed to be worth *£2 million*. The acquisition of this wealth made it possible for her to carry out not only *her own desires* for benefiting the people of Stone and Meaford, but also a *wish of her father, the 2nd Viscount*. As early as 1861 she had, in accordance with this wish, offered to contribute £1500 towards the erection of a *market hall and town hall*, in one building, provided that a further sum of £500 was raised, this sum and £250 of her own contribution to be set aside as a repairing fund. The money was raised, but difficulties arose over the purchase from Earl Granville, the Lord of the Manor, of the old Butter Market.[4] Delays continued until 1867 when it was decided to proceed with the Market Hall as a separate project. The Butter Market was demolished, and the new hall was opened on March 2nd 1869, being twice as large as the previous one. It bore this inscription over the main entrance: "To fulfil the wish of Edward Jervis Jervis, Viscount St. Vincent, this building is erected for the benefit of those who attend Stone Market, A.D. 1868."

In 1862 Mary Anne married George Cecil Weld, who later became the 3rd Lord Forester. Her interest in Stone continued and a site was obtained for the building of a *Town Hall*: this was the "Blue Bell" inn in High St. The building was completed early in 1870, and the opening marked by a public dinner. A newspaper report of 1867[5] had said that "the town itself is suffering, and has been for years, for public room and market accommodation." Both these needs were now satisfied, for the Town Hall in 1870 was an elegant building, with excellent waiting rooms on each side of the entrance, a large hall 60 feet by 34 feet 6 inches "for public concerts, lectures or balls", capable of seating 400 persons, and "at one end is a well-constructed platform". In the rear of the hall were retiring rooms and offices, and over the waiting rooms at the front was a large library and reading room, 36 feet long and 16 feet wide.[6] The estimated cost of the building without fittings was £2,500, towards which Lady Forester contributed £1,500, Mr. George Meakin of the Hayes gave £250 and Mr. Thomas Bostock £200. To the new room at the Town Hall the *Mechanics Institute* transferred its *library of 1500 volumes* from St. Michael's School, and added copies of the London daily papers and monthly periodicals.

Soon after 1873 Lady Forester was able to purchase the Meaford estate, which from then remained in the Parker-Jervis branch of the family. She then built a completely new portion on to the Hall, retaining the ivy-covered portion of the original house in which was the room where Earl St. Vincent was born and his favourite Bow parlour. The new portion was of red brick, and is the only portion now remaining, since the break-up of the Parker-Jervis estate. One of the outstanding features of this new portion was a magnificent staircase of malachite which Lady Forester had brought from Russia. At *Meaford* the inn and estate cottages were rebuilt at her expense in an improved style, and she also built the school, used for divine worship on Sunday afternoons.

Meanwhile, at the *Parish Church*, little had altered, save the installation of gas lighting in 1859, and the Rev. Eldred Woodland's minor improvements. In 1884 the Rev. *Newdigate Poyntz* became rector, and quickly complained that the church was:

". . . deficient in cleanliness, in beauty, in accommodation for the artisan class of which we have a great number in the town, and in accommodation for the choir and clergy . . . the only free seats are the benches in the gallery upon which it would be a penance to sit, and the chairs down the centre of the church, the floor of which is so damp in winter that it is simply shameful to ask any person to kneel upon it."

He suggested a new scheme to lower the seats in the nave, removing the doors; relay the floor where necessary, and instal a hot water apparatus; to lengthen the chancel and build an organ chamber and vestry. The immediate problem of the freehold rights of pew owners caused the plan for improved seating to be dropped. The remainder of the scheme, however, received tremendous impetus when *Lady Forester* announced in July 1886 her intention to build *a new chancel and organ chamber* at the church at a cost of £1500 in memory of her nephew, *the 4th Viscount St. Vincent*, who had been killed at the Battle of Abu Klea in the Sudan.[8] The foundation-stone was laid by Lady Forester's nephew, Mr. W. R. Parker-Jervis, on October 29th 1886, and the work was completed within the year. The chancel remains today very much as it was after this building work; in the nave the wood panelled ceiling took the place of the old plastered one, and the western gallery was removed. The new heating apparatus made it possible to scrap the large stove which had a flue pipe going up to the old ceiling and then out through a window in the north gallery. The east window, given by Mrs. Foden of Edgehill in memory of her husband John (1813-1875) has tracery copied from 15th century examples.[9] Mr. H. Minton-Senhouse gave the tiles for the chancel floor, and Mrs. Meakin of Darlaston Hall gave the brass altar rails and chancel gas-standards. The Jervis family had by this time sold the Darlaston estates, and the Meakin family were living there. The *new chancel* was dedicated on Michaelmas Day 1887 by the Bishop of Lichfield, and at the same service a memorial tablet, erected in honour of *John Edward Leveson Jervis, 4th Viscount St. Vincent*, was unveiled by General Wolseley, K.G., G.C.B., G.C.M.G.

A new organ was presented to the church in 1888 in memory of William Elley Bromley of the Mansion House, Stone, by his widow, and dedicated on September 27th 1888. From this same period of restoration date many of the stained glass windows,[10] which have now replaced all but one of the original plain windows. In 1896 two *bells*, cast by Taylors of Loughborough, were added, thus completing the peal of eight bells, and a new clock was placed in the tower.

At *Christ Church*, too, restoration and improvement were being undertaken between 1884 and 1885. The chancel was rebuilt and refurnished, an organ chamber provided on the north side into which the organ was moved from the west gallery, and vestries were built on the south side.[11] A new pulpit of white stone and alabaster was installed, and to commemorate the Queen's Jubilee in 1897 an octagonal font was provided.[12] There was more work to be done when the Rev. Russell Line became vicar in 1894, and defects were discovered in the twin spires and in the roof. Instead of carrying out the repairs, it was decided to rebuild the nave in order to accommodate 200 more worshippers. Work of demolition began on May 1st 1899, and on June 2nd a new foundation-stone was laid by *Mr. W. R. Parker-Jervis*, grandson of Viscountess St. Vincent, who had laid the first stone. The church was re-opened by the Bishop of Lichfield on October 13th 1900.[13]

In April 1886 the Inspector of Schools had reported that the Christ Church school in the Radfords was "altogether unfit for school purposes, and he could not much longer recommend it being recognised by the Department."[14] *New schools* were built in *Northesk St.* at a cost of £2,900. Contributors included Lady Forester, £1,000; the Duke of Sutherland, £250; the Hon. E. S. Parker-Jervis, £200; Mr. Hamar Bass, M.P., £100; Mrs. Meakin of Darlaston Hall, £100. The schools were opened in 1888 by the Earl of Harrowby; the *Stonefield school*, enlarged in 1881, continued as an infant school.

Great changes were now imminent in the history of the *Grammar School*. Although Mr. Wade had brought great improvements in the new building in Station Rd., many inhabitants in Stone felt, as did the people of Uttoxeter, that the fullest use was not being made of the money which should be available, and a petition was sent to Trinity College and to the Charity Commissioners requesting a new scheme of administration. A scheme for *Stone* was drawn up in November 1886. A capital sum of £3,000 was to be provided for new school buildings suitable for not less than 80 scholars, and capable of extension; a yearly sum of £400 was to be paid to the Governors of the School for its maintenance, and for the salary of the Headmaster, who had to be a graduate; boys of nine years of age upwards could be taken, both boarders and day-boys, and the numbers had to include the holders of eight scholarships entitling them to free tuition for three years.[15] In the award of one half of these scholarships, preference was to be given to boys who were, or for not less than three years, had been pupils of a Public Elementary School in Stone, or within a radius of three miles. A new Governing Body was set up, and at the first meeting in December 1886 Lord Harrowby was appointed Chairman.

From the outset Lord Harrowby realised that the £3,000 from Trinity College would not buy a good site *and* build a school to meet the needs of the town and district. He had found a site of 5½ acres at Oulton Cross which the owner, Mr. Slater, was willing to sell at £230 per acre. The Charity Commissioners refused to sanction a mortgage, or to approve greater expenditure. Lord Harrowby then acted on his own initiative: he wrote a long private letter to *Lady Forester*, dated February 27th 1887, explaining the position and asking for her assistance, even though he himself felt, and wrote, that "it was a very impertinent request to make."[16] Within two days she had asked for a copy of the 1886 scheme "for Willm. Jervis to see and give me his advice upon,"[17] checking every point, especially the fact that, if she gave the site, the whole of the £3,000 would

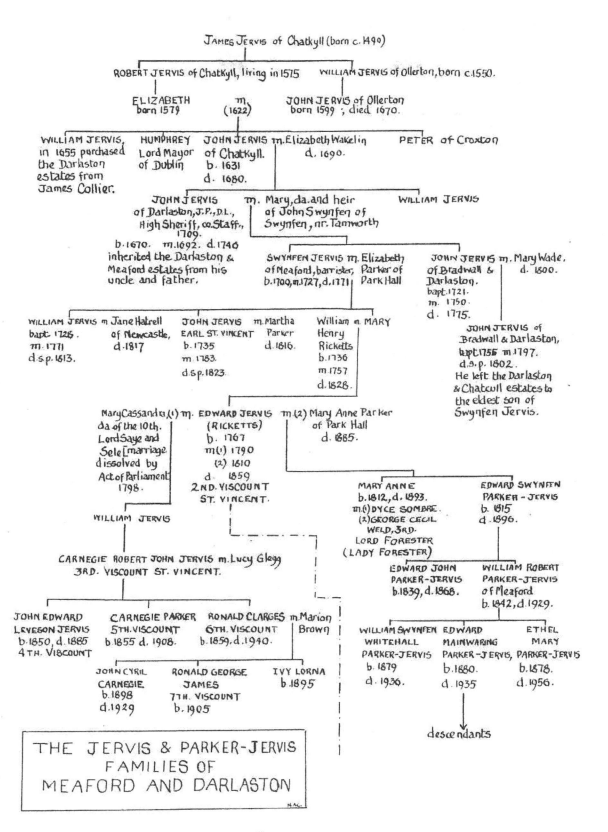

THE JERVIS & PARKER-JERVIS FAMILIES OF MEAFORD AND DARLASTON

JAMES JERVIS of Chatkyll (born c.1490)

ROBERT JERVIS of Chatkyll, living in 1575   WILLIAM JERVIS of Ollerton, born c.1550.

ELIZABETH born 1579   m (1622)   JOHN JERVIS of Ollerton born 1599; died 1670.

WILLIAM JERVIS, in 1655 purchased the Darlaston estates from James Collier.

HUMPHREY Lord Mayor of Dublin

JOHN JERVIS m. Elizabeth Wakelin of Chatkyll. b. 1631 d. 1680.   d. 1690.

PETER of Croxton

JOHN JERVIS of Darlaston, J.P., D.L., High Sheriff, co.Staff., 1709. b. 1670. m. 1692. d. 1746 inherited the Darlaston & Meaford estates from his uncle and father.   m. Mary, da. and heir of John Swynfen of Swynfen, nr. Tamworth

WILLIAM JERVIS

SWYNFEN JERVIS m. Elizabeth of Meaford, barrister, Parker of b. 1700, m. 1727, d. 1771 Park Hall

JOHN JERVIS m. Mary Wade, of Bradwall & d. 1800. Darlaston. bapt. 1721. m. 1750. d. 1775.

WILLIAM JERVIS m Jane Halrell bapt. 1725. of Newcastle. m. 1771 d. 1817. d.s.p. 1813.

JOHN JERVIS m.Martha EARL ST. VINCENT Parker b. 1735 d. 1816. m. 1783. d.s.p. 1823.

William m. MARY Henry Ricketts b. 1736 m. 1757 d. 1828.

JOHN JERVIS of Bradwall & Darlaston, bapt.1755 m.1797. d.s.p. 1802. He left the Darlaston & Chatcull estates to the eldest son of Swynfen Jervis.

Mary Cassandra (1) m. EDWARD JERVIS da of the 10th. (RICKETTS) Lord Saye and b. 1767 Sele [marriage m.(1) 1790 dissolved by (2.) 1810 Act of Parliament] d. 1859 1798.   2ND. VISCOUNT ST. VINCENT.   m.(2) Mary Anne Parker of Park Hall d. 1885.

WILLIAM JERVIS

CARNEGIE ROBERT JOHN JERVIS m. Lucy Glegg 3RD. VISCOUNT ST. VINCENT.

MARY ANNE b. 1812, d. 1893. m.(1) DYCE SOMBRE. (2) GEORGE CECIL WELD, 3RD. LORD FORESTER (LADY FORESTER)

EDWARD SWYNFEN PARKER - JERVIS b. 1815 d. 1896.

JOHN EDWARD LEVESON JERVIS b. 1850, d. 1885 4TH. VISCOUNT

CARNEGIE PARKER 5TH. VISCOUNT b. 1855 d. 1908.

RONALD CLARGES m.Marion 6TH. VISCOUNT Brown b. 1859, d. 1940.

EDWARD JOHN PARKER - JERVIS b. 1839, d. 1868.

WILLIAM ROBERT PARKER - JERVIS of Meaford b. 1842, d. 1929.

JOHN CYRIL CARNEGIE b. 1898 d. 1929

RONALD GEORGE JAMES 7TH. VISCOUNT b. 1905

IVY LORNA b. 1895

WILLIAM SWYNFEN WHITEHALL PARKER-JERVIS b. 1879 d. 1936.

EDWARD MAINWARING PARKER-JERVIS b. 1880. d. 1935

ETHEL MARY PARKER-JERVIS b. 1878. d. 1956.

descendants

PLATE 20

be available for building. On June 4th 1887 Lady Forester sent a short note to Lord Harrowby, enclosing a cheque for £1265, for the

"purchase of the field at Oulton belonging to Mr. Slater, which was recommended by the the Charity Commissioners for the site of the Grammar School. . . . I hope that the honoured name of Thomas Alleyne and the date 1558 will be preserved outside the building."[18]

With this magnificent Oulton Cross site placed at their disposal, the Governors were able to go ahead with building to the plan submitted by Mr. W. Hawley Lloyd of Birmingham[19] . . . "a master's house and school in one group in a style intended to recall some of the character of the period in which Thomas Alleyne lived." The building was completed by the middle of 1889, and officially opened on June 17th by *Earl Granville*, the famous Victorian statesman, and Lord of the Manor of Stone. Under its new head, Mr. Peake, Alleyne's began yet another chapter in its chequered history, and though the prospects were brighter than ever before, success was still not to be gained easily or quickly.

A few years before the opening of the Grammar School, a *disastrous fire* on March 7th 1886 had almost completely destroyed the *Congregational Church*. Presumed to have been due to overheating, the fire started beneath the vestry, then spread to the organ loft and to the rafters of the church on the one side, and of the schoolroom on the other. The flames spread with such rapidity that the whole building was soon ablaze, and the fire could be seen for miles around.[20] The disaster could not have occurred in a worse part of the town, or at a worse time. In bitterly cold weather, and with many nearby pumps frozen, the only adequate water supply was 500 yards away. The firemen did their utmost in conditions which more than once froze the water in the hoses, while water which fell on the lamps outside the schoolroom froze into icicles more than a foot in length. It was five o'clock in the morning before entry into the building was possible: the spire and the outside walls alone remained; everything inside was destroyed. A building which had cost £5,000, and the final debt on which had been cleared two years previously, was destroyed in a few hours. The pastor was the *Rev. William Nicholson:* he and his officers immediately took over the Town Hall for services, and decided to rebuild at once. The schools were re-opened on October 3rd of the same year, and the new church was opened on January 24th 1887, with some improvements, including the raising of the tower by six feet to take a large illuminated *clock* with three faces, the gift of *Mr. Richard Vernon*, shoe manufacturer of Stone.[21] A manse was built next to the church in 1897 at a cost of £1,000 and a Guild room erected adjoining the schools.[22]

During this period, public buildings and churches had been generously and adequately provided. But the rapid and uncontrolled provision of houses for a population which had now more than doubled, brought health problems which had for too long been conveniently ignored. It was that grand old man, *John Ford*, who called a meeting in 1865 to consider the adoption for Stone of the *Local Government Act of 1858*, by which it could have its own duly-constituted governing body. There were, in 1865, twenty-five cases of typhoid fever in the town; bad drainage, open sewers and uncleanliness in the houses, if not the only causes, had greatly aggravated the disease. *Dr. Edward Fernie*, a young and keen practitioner, drew attention to the smell of sewers in the Stonefield area, and warned of the danger of cholera.[23] This first meeting reached no decision, but the young doctor was prepared to go on striving – for years if need be – to remedy the evils of the town. In 1869 he wrote to the local press:[24]

> "Let any of your readers . . . walk up a street by the side of the parish church, down a street leading to the bridge across the Trent, then turn aside into Abbey-court, and afterwards through the Back-lane and High Street, into the Newcastle and Oulton roads, and if he does not see as much and more surface filth, and smell as many and more odours from it, than he ever saw or smelt in any other town of equal size, I shall be very much mistaken. . . . An analysis of water taken from wells situated in different parts of the town and chemically examined in Birmingham showed it to be all more or less polluted by drainage and unfit for domestic use unless previously boiled and filtered."

Still nothing happened! In 1874 *Dr. Ballard*, medical officer of the Local Government Board, came from London to make an on-the-spot investigation. He then made a lengthy report[25] to the *Board of Guardians*, a report described by Dr. Fernie as "severe but true". Although less than 100 years ago, Dr. Ballard found ashpits close to houses, full and in some cases overflowing, simply covered over with a few boards – a condition universal in the lower and poorer part of the town. There were parts of the town where there were no privies at all, and one case where 35 people occupying 5 houses were using one place, which was also accessible to anyone from the road. Goodwin's Hole[26] in Church St. was one of the worst places he had seen in all his experience.

The sewers of the town, so far as they existed, were on no system, and merely took sewage into streams, such as the Scotch Brook; many parts of the town had neither sewage nor drainage.

The water supply of Stone was derived entirely from wells sunk into the ground. Some of these wells were sunk within a yard or two of cesspools, in porous soil, and pollution from this source was aggravated by the fact that many of the grids used to take away waste water were close to wells. In some cases the waste filth ran into a wide trench within a couple of yards of a well. The absence of sewage and drainage, bad position and polluted condition of the wells, were universal throughout the Stone district.

The blame was placed squarely on the Board of Guardians who, after the Public Health Act of 1872, had been the authority for sanitary purposes. They had failed to appoint a medical officer of health, they had had fever in the town for a whole year, but had failed to ascertain the number of cases, or call in medical advice. Dr. Ballard listed the remedies: a *medical officer* must be appointed; the town must be *efficiently sewered*, and the sewage properly disposed of, not turned into the canal or the river, and an ample supply of *pure water* must be obtained. "Whatever the cost, all thus must be done."

A lot more haggling by the Guardians followed. "They do nothing but talk", accused Dr. Ballard, whose second report in January 1875 stated that "nothing had been done to improve the water supply of Stone . . .no improvement had been effected in the sewerage or drainage of the town."

More talking and the finding of all sorts of difficulties were cut short by a Local Government Inspector who, in March 1877, suggested the *making of Stone into a special drainage district*. The boundaries of the town were agreed upon, tenders for a scheme of drainage were sought, and a loan of £5,000 for the work was arranged. A public meeting on March 12th gave the plan overwhelming support, and on May 29th 1878 the Local Government Board came into being. Elections were held, nine members appointed, and Dr. Fernie was made Chairman during the first three years.

Under this new authority improvements were steadily carried out: sanitation, drainage, lighting and re-surfacing of the streets. The disastrous fire at the Congregational Church had emphasised the need for an adequate water-supply in all parts of the town. In February 1888 a start was made on the drilling of a bore-hole near the Rockwood; by September a depth of 500 feet had been reached, and over a month's trial pumping the temporary apparatus gave an average yield of 180,000 gallons a day. The whole project was completed by March 1890 when Stone had a reservoir holding 300,000 gallons of pure water, at a height (on the Red Hill) of 300 feet above the level of the Market Square, and with a pressure sufficient for the top storey of any house in the town.[28]

NOTES AND REFERENCES

1. See plate 19.
2. See plate 20.
3. See a) Dictionary of National Biography.
    b) Notes & Queries, 8th series, vol. vii., pp. 310–311.
    c) ibid. p. 375.
    d) Annual Register, 1851 (Chronicle, p. 303).
4. See plate 10.
5. Staffordshire Advertiser, 21 September 1867.
6. ibid. 26 February 1870.
7. J. R. Booth: Stone, Links with the Past, pp. 15–19.
8. Staffordshire Advertiser, 3 July 1886.
9. The window was the work of Ward and Hughes of London.
10. For details see Norman A. Cope: History and Guide to Stone Parish Church (St. Michael).
11. Staffordshire Advertiser, 21 February 1885 and 28 February 1885.
12. ibid. 23 April 1887.
13. J. R. Booth: Stone: Links with the Past, pp. 47–49.
14. Staffordshire Advertiser, 17 April 1886.
15. Scheme of 1886, par. 22.

16. From the original correspondence preserved at Alleyne's School.
17. As above, written on the back of an envelope.
18. From the original correspondence.
19. Birmingham Post, 18 July 1889. See Plate 18.
20. Staffordshire Advertiser, 13 March 1886.
21. ibid. 29 January 1887.
22. ibid. 26 June 1897 and 26 March 1898.
23. ibid. 14 October 1865.
24. ibid. 13 November 1869.
25. ibid. 24 January 1874.
26. Also known as Goblin's Hole: a row of earlier houses, below the level of the present Church St. houses, on the "Robin Hood" side.
27. Staffordshire Advertiser, 9 January 1875.
28. ibid. 15 March 1890.

Pump Square, around the year 1890. The town pump is in the centre. Between the shop of Charles E. Babb and the Temperance Hotel is the Pirehill & Meaford Savings Bank. The Post Office is next to the District Bank.

Granville Square, about 1916, after the pump had been removed, and a shrubbery (including a young plane tree) had been erected as a memorial of the coronation of King Edward VII.

Plate   21

CHAPTER 15

"THE OLD ORDER CHANGETH"

Even though the Local Board were now responsible for the town of Stone, the care of the poor remained in the hands of the Guardians, and they continued the management of the *Workhouse*. Ale for the inmates was brewed on the premises until 1876, when it was put out to contract. In 1884 the Guardians ordered a 42s. cask of ale, most of which was consumed on Christmas Day. The Poor Law Auditor found that this allowed 4½ pints to each man, and 3½ pints to each woman in the workhouse, and half the cost of the ale was surcharged to the Guardians themselves.[1]

The Guardians were criticised, too, for the "idleness which prevailed among the able-bodied inmates."[2] In Mr. Adie's time as master, the making of mops and mats, spinning and other work was carried on; this had now ceased, and it was thought that the breaking of stone for road-making would be a suitable and useful occupation. It was 1904 before the Guardians made provision for this, as a means of controlling the increasing number of vagrants using the casual wards.[3]

In the town the *Local Board* continued its work of improvement right up to 1895, in which year the *Urban District Council* came into being under the Local Government Act of 1894. In 1892 the Board had made plans for a complete sewerage scheme, with works between the Canal and the River Trent, and by the end of 1895 it was stated that

"the sanitary conditions of Stone have been greatly improved, and a notable decrease in the death rate has taken place since the old authority was so soundly rated by Dr. Ballard for its neglect."[4]

By 1911 filter beds and a refuse destructor had been built,[5] and the sewage works were shortly afterwards completed at a cost of £9,000.[6] This new sewage scheme at last made it possible to adopt the water-carriage system in place of the old objectionable tub-system, and in order to be quite sure of adequate water supplies, improvements were carried out at the Waterworks, costing £3,000.

It must have been heart-breaking for Stone in 1895, having gone a long way towards "putting its own house in order", to find industrial waste from works in the Potteries being turned into the River Trent, with disastrous results. Previous to this, the *Trent* used to afford capital fishing, big pike at Darlaston and trout at almost any point, but especially below Walton Bridge. The waste, believed by some to have come from Etruria Gasworks, killed tons of fish near Stone. Quantities were raked out in a dying condition, and sold around the town from handcarts, but when cooked all the fish tasted of tar, and were unfit to eat.

The next problem for the Urban Council was that of space for burials. In the 1890s Dr. Fernie, the medical officer of health, had warned that both St. Michael's and Christ Church burial grounds would soon be full[7] and in 1898 an Inspector from the Home Office visited Stone,[8] and an Order in Council was made on

February 2nd 1899 closing both churchyards after the end of 1900, with a few exceptions about existing vaults. This forced the Council's hand, and, even though the effective date of the order was postponed, a 4 acre site for a cemetery was acquired on the Stafford Rd. The necessary buildings were erected, and the cemetery was opened on September 5th 1903. The total cost had been £3,100.[9]

In 1904 the *Stone Fire Brigade* had come under the control of the *Stone Fire Engines Joint Committee*, but this did not impair the efficiency and enthusiasm of the service, encouraged by annual competitions. Following the purchase of the "Edith Mabel" steamer, other appliances were added and by 1889 the brigade had been described as "efficient as anyone could wish, and the fire station would bear comparison with anything within fifty miles of Stone."[10] A great number of long-service medals were awarded, many for 20 and 25 years' service, proof of loyalty to a voluntary organisation. In 1924 the brigade acquired its first motor fire-engine, supplied by Merryweather & Sons.

Various attempts had been made around this period to revive the enthusiasm of the old wakes. In 1883 the Local Board had approved of side-shows and other amusements being brought into the High St. at holiday times such as Christmas, Easter, Whitsuntide and the Wakes. Mr. "Booty" Turner,[11] who had a shop in Stafford St. and who made boots and clogs for the boat people on the canal as well as for workers in the town, did much to revive the old Wakes fairs, and the last one was held on the old race-course. Later on, the amusements centred on Pat Ganley's Field, or the *Wakes' Field*, now Stonefield Park; to this same field came "Snape's 3d. Gaff", a travelling theatre which would stay for three months at a time, giving dramatic performances every evening. In Pump Square *Wombwell's Menagerie* used to set up a show, displaying wild animals, birds and reptiles, "the like of which had never been seen before". St. Michael's School log-book records on September 19th 1881: "A menagerie stopping in the town today, a very thin attendance." *Lord George Sanger's Circus* was another attraction, loudly proclaiming its arrival by a parade through the main street, the appeal of which defeated the most rigorous of schoolmasters:

"1881. 30th May. Poor attendance. Circus in afternoon.
Compelled to give holiday in consequence.

1889. 14th October. This afternoon the school had a half-holiday on account of Sanger's circus being in the town."[12]

Another feature was the *Christmas Mummers' or Guisers' play* of St. George, last performed in the town in 1897. The players were dressed in any fantastic finery they could get—white and coloured calico, ribbons and paper. They wore cardboard helmets, and were armed with wooden swords. The hero of the play was St. George, and his opponents were various—Slasher, the Prince of Paradise, and Bold Old Ben, and there was a 'doctor' who tried to revive the wounded. The prologue introduced the play[13] with these words:

> "I open the door, I enter in,
> I hope your favour for to win;
> Whether I rise, stand or fall,
> I'll do my best to please you all.
> Stir up the fire to make a light,
> To see these merry actors fight."

After St. George had recounted his prowess, he was challenged by Slasher to fight. In the ensuing tussle Slasher was wounded, and the King of Egypt entered:

> "Alas, alas, my chiefest son is slain,
> What shall I do to raise him up again?
> Here he lies in the presence of you all,
> I should loudly like for a doctor to be called."

A doctor appeared, and was closely questioned about his ability, and his cures: the following conversation then ensued:

KING OF EGYPT: How far has thou travelled to be such a noble doctor?

DOCTOR: From Italy, Titaly, Germany, France and Spain, and now returned to cure diseases in old England again.

KING OF EGYPT: So far and no farther?

DOCTOR: O yes, and a great deal further: from the fireside to the cupboard door upstairs and into bed.

KING OF EGYPT: What diseases canst thou cure?

DOCTOR: All sorts.

KING OF EGYPT: What is all sorts?

DOCTOR: The itch, the pitch, the palsy and the gout.
> If a man's got nineteen devils in his skull,
> I can cast twenty of them out.
> I have in my pocket crutches for lame ducks,
> Spectacles for blind bumble bees,
> And plasters for broken-backed mice.
> I cured St. Harry of an agony about 150 yards long,
> And surely I can cure this poor man.
> Here Jack, take a little pull out of my bottle
> And let it run down thy throttle;
> And if thou be'est not quite slain,
> Rise up, Jack, and fight again."

Slasher revived for a moment, then died. The Prince of Paradise took up the challenge, and he too was slain. Bold Old Ben planned to fight with St. George at some other time and place, but was cleared away by Beelzebub, who said:

> "Here am I, old Beelzebub,
> And in my hand I carry my club,
> And on my shoulder a dripping pan.

I think myself a jolly old man.
Down in yonder meadow, where the birds sing funny,
Ladies and gentlemen, please fill my ladle with money.
My ladle's dumb, and cannot speak,
So, fill it full for St. George's sake."

On a more serious note, it was the custom, shortly before the end of the 19th century, for people requiring servants to live in, both male and female, to hire them at Christmas time, at a hiring fair called *Gorby's market*, for the term of one year, at the end of which they were sent away, although often re-engaged: this was done to prevent them getting a settlement in the parish.[14]

The uncertainty of work in those days was not confined to servants, for the town was largely dependent on *the shoe trade* for employment, and this industry was very liable to seasonal slackness of trade. The difficulties for families were often quite serious, as these examples show:

"1879. Feb. 24th Little or no improvement in the trade of the town. Much distress prevails. School fees paid with great irregularity. Useless to send the children back, in the majority of cases, as the parents are not earning wherewith to pay."[15]

Distress was again widespread in 1892:

"Slackness of trade still continues and at present there does not appear to be much prospect of improvement . . . orders are not to hand, and in the present uncertain state of the market manufacturers cannot work for stock. . . . The hard weather which set in this week gave the Local Board an opportunity to set about 50 of the unemployed men at work cleaning away the heavy fall of snow. Much has been done lately by private benevolence towards mitigating the distress."[16]

A relief fund had, indeed, been operating all winter. Between October 1892 and March 1893 the committee had distributed 8,645 loaves, 202 tons of coal, and 1767 pounds of meat. During the last fortnight of the period 250 gallons of soup had been provided.[17]

When trade was normal, shoemaking employed between 2000 and 3000 of the inhabitants of Stone and its neighbourhood, and the products of Stone factories were known the world over. Messrs. Bostocks, the largest producers, had a large trade with Australia, especially in the better quality lines; the New Zealand trade was growing, and in South Africa the Stone goods were competing successfully with the smarter-looking Austrian products, and with those made in North America. The firm known as the Richard Vernon Boot and Shoe Company had such a substantial trade with Melbourne in Australia that, when he retired, Mr. Vernon built "Melbourne House" in Mount Rd. Other small factories were those of Lewis and Adie, Lewis and Johnson, and Tomlinson's, this last one situated behind Gundry's shop in High Street. There was also the factory of Charles Bromley, who prepared his own leather in the tanyards in Crown St.[18] For the smaller factories, however, the writing was on the wall, with competition becoming ever keener, and in 1905 Mr. Harry Price expressed the opinion[19] that the large factories would become larger and the smaller ones would be forced out of business.

Joule's Brewery also had a considerable export trade to Australia, New Zealand and California; as many as 400 hogsheads went to Melbourne in one consignment. The company founded by John Joule was taken over in 1870 by Mr. Thomas Harding and Mr. John Parrington of Liverpool, and became a limited company in 1898. The trade name of "Stone Ale" was made the sole copyright of the company, following a law-suit taken to the House of Lords in 1888; the company was also permitted to use a red cross as its trade-mark, provided it was always shown on a green background, to avoid contravention of the cross used by the International Red Cross Organisation. The old *brickyard* in Mount Rd. (Beech's brickyard) produced many of the bricks used in building the Stonefield houses. After the yard closed a Mr. Montgomery of Liverpool built nearby the *New Brewery* or Montgomery's Brewery, which later became *Bent's Brewery*, and which is now closed.

In the 1890s prices of goods were amazingly low by comparison with today: 4d. for a 4-lb. loaf; cheese 2½d. to 4½d. a lb.; bacon 3d. and 4d; sugar 1¼d. to 1½d. a lb.; four tallow candles cost 1d.; best farm butter was 6d. to 8d. a lb.; best boiled ham, 1s. 4d. to 1s. 6d. a lb.; fresh milk was 1d. a pint in summer and 1½d. in winter; skimmed milk was 1½d. a quart. A dozen boxes of matches cost 2d. and the best brands of tobacco 4d. an ounce. A tailor-made suit, guaranteed to last years, was 50s., and a ready-made one was 25s.; best boots 10s. a pair, others as low as 3s. 9d.; a cap was 6d., a pair of corduroy trousers 5s. 6d., while rough slack was 4½d. a hundredweight, and coke could be had for 4d. a barrow from the gas-works if you filled it yourself. Whisky was 3s. 6d. a bottle, Guiness stout 1s. 9d. a dozen, strong beer 1s. 6d. a gallon and light beer 1s. 1d. But against these prices had to be set the fact that skilled labour wages were about £1. 8s. a week, and unskilled 16s. to £1.[20]

The *Stone Nursing Association* had been founded in 1876, and in 1899 the Stone Joint Hospital Board installed disinfecting apparatus at *Yarnfield Isolation Hospital*. In 1908 the foundation stone of a *new Isolation Hospital* was laid, so that the original hospital could be used for smallpox cases only. The larger hospitals were still mainly dependent on voluntary support, and in 1891 Mr. S. Perry began the *Hospital Saturday* collections to raise funds for the Staffordshire General and North Staffordshire Infirmaries. The Friendly Societies were also continuing their work, backed by the medical profession, Dr. *Fallows* was the Oddfellows' surgeon back in 1842, and in 1863 Dr. *Fernie*[21] succeeded him in that capacity. The number of members in 1863 was 113 with a capital of £1000; in 1905 the membership was 557 with funds of £10,000.[22]

In 1884 the *Post Office* moved from its corner site in Pump Square to premises on the lower side of the District Bank;[23] the postmaster was *William Biddulph Woolley*, who had held the post since 1864 and who retired in 1904. He was a deacon of the Congregational Church for 59 years. The premises vacated by the

Post Office were opened in 1889 by Mr. *C. E. Babb* as a draper's: children's stockings were 2½d. a pair; women's stockings 3½d. a pair; flannelette 2¾d. a yard and calico 2d. Good towels were 4½d. each and sheets 2s. 11d. a pair. Ladies' coats were 12s. 6d. each. The business progressed and in 1890 a baby-linen department was opened behind the shop; by 1894 Elsmore's crockery shop on the Pump Square side was incorporated, and then Stephens' chemists in Radford St. This shop, further developed, remained as a family business until very recently, when it was taken over by Woodall's.

In 1890 the "new system of *telephonic communication* between London and the business centres of the provinces was rapidly being perfected. The trunk line of the National Telephone Company had reached Stone. To the continuation of this line Stafford would be connected . . . and a scheme was on foot to connect the Chief Constable's office at Stafford with the police officers in all the towns in Staffordshire that used the telephone . . . the first being Bilston, Brierley Hill, West Bromwich, Wednesbury, Stoke-on-Trent, Burslem, Longton, Stone and Burton-on-Trent.[24]

The *Mechanics' Institute*, now established at the Town Hall, had 150 members in 1895, and there were also classes for science under Mr. T. W. Berry; art classes under Mr. J. W. Clough, and classes in boot and shoe making. Another aspect of the Institute's work was the *Penny Reading :* the more talented citizens would give their individual performances, free of charge, before their fellow members, and, during the intervals refreshments were served, a cup of tea or coffee for a penny, with penny cakes. In 1899 the Urban Council decided that, in order to bring technical education into line with educational policy, a *Technical Instruction Committee* should be set up, and this committee launched its first season of classes in September 1903:

Classes in boot and shoe making, and joinery, in Westbridge House.[25]
Book-keeping and commercial classes at St. Michael's School.
Shorthand and Typewriting at Christ Church Schools.
Art classes at the Mechanics' Institute.
French classes at St. Dominic's School.[26]

These scattered classes worked very well for a number of years, but not well enough, and in 1908 the County Education Committee decided to build a centre for instruction in cookery, laundry, handicrafts &c. and three years later the *Kitchener Institute* was opened.

Throughout the period from 1858 the *Volunteer movement* had continued with undiminished enthusiasm. In 1878 there was a change from the "Glengarry", previously worn, to the regulation helmet, a more Prussian-like head-gear with a spike on top. Two years later, letters were substituted for numbers, and Stone became "L" company. When *Captain Bromley* retired through ill-health in 1886,[27] Captain Harding continued the excellent work of the corps. In 1897 the Stone Company won the 1st. national prize of £30 in the competition of the Field-Firing Association.[28] and repeated the success the following year.

CHRIST CHURCH IN 1841, based on a drawing by J.C.Buckler.
(Brit. Mus. Add. Mss. 36387, f. 240.)

STONE PARISH CHURCH (ST. MICHAEL'S) IN 1841, SHOWING THE JERVIS
FAMILY MAUSOLEUM, also based on a drawing by J.C.Buckler.
(Brit. Mus. Add. Mss. 36387, f. 237)

PLATE 22.

Excellent work had gone into the training of the corps by men like Col. Sergeant Harris, bandmaster Henry Wood, Sergt. Instructor Mulvial, Corpl. T. Harris and Quartermaster Sergt. Sampson Hodson, so that when the Boer War commenced in October 1899 there was no lack of efficient volunteers in Stone eager to join the reservists of the 2nd. North Stafford Regiment who left for South Africa on December 27th. By the time the war ended on May 31st 1902, a total of 120 men from Stone had served in the war. After conditions of peace had again been restored, the Company held a large fete in July 1903 in Darlaston Park, which raised over £200 to provide the volunteer band with a new set of instruments. The volunteer movement in its old form was now almost finished; in 1908 the volunteers became the *Territorial Army*, Stone being "F" company, 5th Battalion of the North Staffordshire Regiment. The strength at the time of the change was 77, under Major J. L. Meakin. By the end of the year, when Lieut. Ridgway took over, the number rose to 90, and by October 1909 it had risen to 103.[29]

There was plenty of sport taking place in Stone during this period. *Football* was being played on the Vine Field in Oulton Rd., where *Stone Town* team were a force to be reckoned with. In 1894 the *Cricket Club* had taken land in Lichfield Rd.,[30] where the club still plays, and in 1905 joined the North Staffs Cricket League. The same year of 1894 saw the start of *athletics* in the town,[31] and the first meeting under A.A.A. laws and N.C.U. rules was held on the football field on August 2nd, when 70 competitors took part. To add to the attractions of this meeting, the Volunteer Band played selections of music in the afternoon, and in the evening played for dancing. These athletic sports grew to be an outstanding event, and in 1903 when A. F. Duffey, world champion, took part, the newspaper comment was:

"The very finest sports held in the country this year! That is not our verdict, it is the opinion of those better qualified to judge. Athlete after athlete came to the Stone officials and congratulated them on the splendid array of talent. Such a band of star performers had not been seen out in any one place this year. Travelled pathmen like Duffey, Wadsley, Hiles, Murray and scores of others were simply amazed not only at the programme, but at the way the competitors turned out."[33]

The sports of 1904 saw the visit of Alfred Shrubb, of South London Harriers, holder of the two miles record.[34] An agreement, in 1909, was made between the Cricket Club and the Athletic Club, whereby the ground was enlarged, and a pavilion and dressing rooms were built;[35] this meant better sport, and in that year not only did Reg. E. Walker, fastest runner in the world at that time, take part, but the meeting was selected to decide the Hurdle Championship of the Midlands.[36]

The *Horticultural Society*, after holding its show in Christ Church vicarage field, had moved to Darlaston Park in 1873. The shows here were probably best remembered as musical treats, for during the years the shows ran, the following famous regimental bands appeared: H.M. Coldstream Guards and Grenadier Guards, Royal Horse Guards, Band and Pipers of H.M. Scots Guards, and the Band of the 2nd Dragoon Guards (Queen's Bays).

For winter evenings there were entertainments at the Town Hall: visits of the Livermore Brothers, the "Christy Minstrels" and the "Burgess Minstrels", all playing to capacity audiences. Stone also had its own *Amateur Minstrel Troupe*, numbering about 20 performers, along with Wood's string band.[37] There was also a *Stone Amateur Operatic and Dramatic Society*,[38] and by 1912 the early silent films reached Stone, when *Mr. G. B. Haddon* formed the Stone Cinema Company and obtained a lease of the Town Hall. In Abbey-street a *Workingmen's Club* had been functioning for some time, but required new and better premises. In 1911 the foundation stones were laid of a new Hall in Lichfield St., which was placed in the hands of Trustees, and the management deputed to a committee of the *St. Michael's Workingmen's Club*. Shortly before the first world war a similar type of club had been established by the Roman Catholic community at *St. Joseph's Hall*, and Christ Church had the *Institute*, using the old school premises in the Radfords.

In 1909 it was reported that the main street of Stone had undergone a complete transformation, several new shops having been opened. There were also signs of the revival of the roads, neglected since the coaching days. The first *cycles* (the bone-shakers) had appeared on the roads as early as 1869. Joe Bloor of Enson had a bone-shaker, and William Mellor of Stone had a Penny-Farthing. The next development was the "safety-bicycle" with solid rubber tyres at first, and then with pneumatic tyres. It was not long before the petrol driven car arrived, and in 1896 the law was revoked which had required the vehicle to be preceded by a herald with a red flag. With the motor car came the complaints, this one as early as 1907:

"The speed of the motor-car, and also that of the motor-cycle, through Stone, will soon have to be considered by the authorities. In addition to kicking up dust, the inhabitants occasionally run the risk of being knocked down, and sometimes accidents are narrowly averted. We don't want the motorist to ignore the town. He is welcome at all times, but we expect his car to be driven at the regulation speed.[39] Lichfield has already taken action with regard to the speed of motors. On Sunday last one car passed along the Lichfield Rd. from Stone at the rate of thirty miles an hour. At this rate the car is dangerous to the public."[40]

By 1912 *Joule's Brewery* were using lorries for the delivery of beer: lorries with solid tyres, without a windscreen, and with oil lamps. A year later, on October 18th 1913, the *"first flying machine"* arrived in Stone, piloted by Gustav Hamel, an event arranged by Messrs. Evans & Sons, garage proprietors, of High St., only four years after Bleriot had flown across the Channel.

The final break with the old order had come in 1903 with the removal of the Town Pump from Pump Square, and the adoption of the new name of Granville Square. As a means of commemorating the coronation of King Edward VII a small enxlosure of shrubs, surrounding a young plane tree, was established in the square.[41] Shortly after the work was completed, an old resident went to the railway station to meet her son, who for some years past, had been working in Leicester. The son duly arrived, and they started to walk home together. In Granville Square the son stopped abruptly:

"Why, mother, where's the pump?"

'It's gone'', said the old lady sadly.

"Well, well', said the lad with a sigh, "the last thing Tom Jones said to me when I left Leicester was, 'Be sure and shake hands with the old pump for me'." Then looking around at the shrubbery he said, "Well, you've made him a pretty grave."[42]

NOTES AND REFERENCES

1. Staffordshire Advertiser, 31 May 1884.
2. ibid. 7 February 1885.
3. ibid. 31 December 1904.
4. ibid. 28 December 1895.
5. Kelly: Staffordshire Directory of 1932 and Stone Weekly News, 30 July 1909.
6. Stone Weekly News, 5 December 1909.
7. Staffordshire Advertiser, 20 February 1897.
8. ibid. 29 January 1898.
9. Stone Weekly News, 13 February 1903 and 11 September 1903.
10. Staffordshire Advertiser, 5 October 1889. The fire station was then behind the Market Hall (now The Library).
11. Stone and Eccleshall Advertiser, 5 September 1957.
12. St. Michael's School log-books.
13. For the full text of the play, see "Folk-Lore of North Staffordshire" by W. Wells Bladen (N.S. Field Club Trans. vol. xxxv (1900–1901) pp. 133–185).
14. N.S. Field Club Trans. vol. xxxv (1900–1901) p. 159, and Arnold Bennett: Jock-at-a-Venture, from Matador of the Five Towns and other Stories, 1912.
15. St. Michael's School log-books.
16. Staffordshire Advertiser, 10 December 1892.
17. ibid. 18 March 1893.
18. Now part of the Stafford St. car-park.
19. Stone Weekly News, 5 May 1905.
20. Staffordshire Advertiser, 22 August 1957.
21. Dr. Fernie died in 1909; there is a commemorative plate in Christ Church.
22. Stone Weekly News, 17 February 1905.
23. The old Post Office is now Lloyd's Bank.
24. Staffordshire Advertiser, 25 January 1890.
25. Formerly the Canal Company's head office.
26. Stone Weekly News, 29 January 1904.
27. Memorial tablet to Captain Bromley in St. Michael's Church.
28. Staffordshire Advertiser, 11 December 1897.
29. Stone Weekly News, 8 October 1909.
30. Staffordshire Advertiser, 3 November 1905.
31. ibid. 2 June 1894.
32. ibid. 4 August 1894.
33. Stone Weekly News, 7 August 1903.
34. ibid. 12 August 1904.
35. ibid. 1 January 1909.
36. ibid. 30 July 1909.
37. Staffordshire Advertiser, 12 May 1894.
38. ibid. 2 February 1905.
39. A speed limit of 20 mph came into force with the Act of 1903, and remained in force until 1930.
40. Stone Weekly News, 17 May 1907.
41. Staffordshire Advertiser, 2 January 1904.
42. Stone Weekly News, 21 August 1903.

CHAPTER 16

TWO WORLD WARS

When the Territorials were formed in 1908 to replace the Volunteers, the intention was that they should be used for home defence, while the regular army would, in case of war, suffice for offensive action. Part of the *Territorial army* training was a fortnight in camp each summer, and on August 1st 1914 the Stone Company, under Captain Ridgway, had gone to St. Asaph in North Wales with the 5th North Staffs Battalion. At 1 a.m. on August 3rd a "stand-to" was ordered, and on the 4th Britain was at war. The Territorials volunteered, almost to a man, for foreign service, and within a few days had left for special training at Luton.[1] On April 1st 1915 the 5th North[2] took over a line of trenches in France, and formed part of the famous 46th division. Censorship made real news of the fighting fronts very scarce, but in letters home they were able to tell of trenches within 30 yards of the German lines, of the first poison gas, and of men waist-deep in mud and water. But from all the fronts, the letters were always cheerful: from Ypres, the Dardanelles and the battle of Mons and subsequent retreat. The greatest blow to the town in war casualities came in the autumn of 1915 with the action against the *Hohenzollern Redoubt*. On September 13th 700 men of the 5th North went into the attack; 500 of them were killed or wounded. On October 27th the Urban District Council paid tribute to the gallantry of the Stone men serving with the battalion, and expressed sympathy with the relatives and friends of the casualities.

Throughout the first world war the demand was constantly for more men. Even though Stone had 450 men in uniform by Christmas 1914, repeated *recruiting campaigns* were held, and the first tribunal under the Derby scheme met in Stone in February 1916. At this same time street lights were extinguished and house-lights screened as a precaution against air-attack, and an air-raid hooter was fixed at Joule's brewery. The *Volunteer movement* was also revived in 1916: men unfit for service abroad or above military age were enrolled. Stone had a platoon of 50 men who drilled regularly, and had camps at Brocton. In the crisis year of 1918 some of them spent six months on home defence work on the east coast.

At the beginning of the war the local *Red Cross Society* was well prepared, for a Stone detachment had been formed in 1913; all members had passed the first aid and nursing examinations, and were ready within a month of the outbreak of hostilities to equip and staff buildings as hospitals. *St. Joseph's Hall* was approved, and in January 1915 a completely voluntary staff was ready to receive convalescent patients from other hospitals.[3] *Miss Meakin* was an indefatigable and enthusiastic commandant, ably supported by *Miss C. H. Knight* as quartermaster. In June 1916 St. Joseph's Hall was converted to a hospital for wounded soldiers,[4] and from that time until the middle of April 1917, 402 soldiers had passed through. By May 1918 the demand for hospital beds had become so acute that Stone Red Cross was asked to extend the accommodation. *Stonefield House*[5] in Newcastle Rd. was placed at the disposal of the local committee, rent free, by Mr. and Mrs.

W. C. Stubbs, and by the first week in June this was a working hospital with 24 beds. For the last six months of war, Stone Red Cross detachment, with a membership now of 60, was running two hospitals entirely with voluntary workers.

The staff of the hospitals were publicly thanked in 1920, when the accounts were closed, Miss Meakin, Miss Knight and Dr. E. F. Fernie being specially mentioned.[6] The self-sacrifice of *Miss Meakin*, who had been responsible for over 1000 patients in four years, was acknowledged by the award of the M.B.E.

Stone had also made early provision for *Belgian refugees*,[7] thanks to *Miss E. M. Parker-Jervis* and a small committee. When the first party of 12 (two families) reached Stone on October 1st 1914 a home on the canal side awaited them, rent free and completely furnished by the people of Stone, and with sufficient funds besides to keep the refugees for a year. A month later a third family was established in Station Rd., and even school-children joined their parents in providing garments for refugees.[8]

On November 24th the saddest party of all arrived:[9] 14 nuns, belonging to the Irish Dames of Ypres, with their Abbess, reached the safety of Oulton Abbey. Driven out by the shelling and the near-destruction of Ypres, the nuns (three of them Belgian, the remainder of them English or Irish) had been travelling for three weeks with their Abbess, who was of great age and paralysed.[10] For this work with the Belgian refugees, and her work with the Sandon Hall Red Cross Hospital, Miss Parker-Jervis was awarded the O.B.E.

Towards the end of 1917 the *food situation* was becoming critical, and a Local Food Committee was established at Westbridge House. Sugar was now rationed, and meat prices fixed. In April 1918 the fixing of milk prices caused a strike of Stone milk retailers (with a few exceptions). For three weeks the committee distributed milk from depots spaced about the town, and the Town Crier was used to keep the public informed of developments. The climax was approaching: more men and more money were needed for the final effort. Each town was given a quota of money to raise: Stone's *Tank Week* target was £15,000. Between March 18th and 23rd 1918 *the town raised 46,500*.[11]

The armistice in November virtually ended the war, but it was July 1919 before *peace celebrations*[12] were held in the town, and it was 1921 when the *war memorial* in Granville Square,[13] designed by Albert Toft, was unveiled by Lord Dartmouth. The tablets record the names of 126 men of Stone, Darlaston and Meaford who gave their lives. It should never be forgotten that out of a population of 5,000, a total of 1100 men had served in the armed forces, nor that the voluntary organisations in the town had risen to meet every demand made upon them.

Between the two world wars, the town of Stone developed considerably. *Houses* were built in Meakin Avenue, Field Terrace and on the Parson's Field between Old Rd. and Oulton Rd., and on the Coppice estate. There was also some *industrial development*: Taylor, Tunnicliff & Co. established electrical porcelain works, the Cauldon Tile Company built a factory in the Filleybrooks, and the Gilt Edge Safety Glass Company developed premises in Mill St. All these new

Granville Square, about 1925, showing the old Crown and Anchor inn, which was gutted by fire in 1937.

The High Street, about 1932, with the old thatched Black Horse Inn on the left.

Plate 23

industries served to diversify the pattern of employment and lessen the risk of slackness in trade.

The urban authority launched a public electricity undertaking; it converted the old Wakes Field into Stonefield Park, and, in 1932, the town's boundaries were *extended* to include Walton, Little Stoke and the Common Plot. To meet the demand of an ever-growing population, new sewage works, costing some £50,000 were designed and commenced before the outbreak of the second world war; in spite of the war, these works were vital and had to be completed; they were opened in 1942.

Long before then, however, war clouds had been gathering over Europe, and local authorities in Britain were forced to consider preparations for the protection of their citizens. By the end of 1937 a skeleton air-raid scheme had been prepared for Stone, and between Munich and the outbreak of war in 1939 the number of volunteers had risen to 500. The town then had a public services team available, a first-aid post set up at St. Dominic's convent, and a control centre for both urban and rural districts in readiness at the Town Hall. Isolated bombs had fallen in the Stone area at the end of June 1940, but it was in the mutual aid calls that the value of the local organisations was realised. In the early hours of November 15th the *Stone rescue team* were at work in the *blitzed city of Coventry*, and on the same day a gas mains repair party from Stone was also in Coventry. Five days later the rescue squad were working in *Birmingham*.

Stone Fire Station was the Headquarters for urban and rural areas, and there were trailer pumps distributed throughout the area, often being towed at first behind private cars. In 1941, when the National Fire Service was formed, *Pirehill Hall* became Fire Force Headquarters for Shropshire and much of Staffordshire, and is today the nerve-centre of the Staffordshire County Fire Service. The Stone brigade gave mutual aid to Birmingham on three occasions, and before D-day personnel from Stone moved to the south coast to help counter air attacks on troop concentrations.

Civil Defence workers were helped by a mobile canteen, manned day and night by the local Women's Voluntary Service, who also ran a canteen for members of H. M. Forces from 1940 until March 1946, led by Lady Johnson and Miss Parker-Jervis.

During the war years, about *800 men and women* served in the armed forces. They were with the army at Dunkirk, Singapore, North Africa, and with the Liberation armies from the Normandy beaches to the end of hostilities; they were with Wingate's Chindits in Burma and in the Arnhem landings. Air Force men, some 125 of them, were not only on the ground and in the Royal Air Force Regiment, but also flying with bombers and fighters, and with Ferry Command. The 60 or so men with the Royal Navy served in submarines, destroyers, boom defence ships, carriers, battleships and mine-sweepers. There were a number of men in the Fleet Air Arm, and some twenty girls were in the women's services and forces' nursing services.

Christmas comforts were sent to the forces each year, though knitted garments could not be sent after 1941 owing to a serious shortage of wool. A *Prisoners of War Fund* was inaugurated and affiliated to Hugh Irving's North Staffs P. O. W. organisation. Stone became responsible for the cost of the monthly parcels sent out through the Stoke packing station to Stone men; donations were also sent to the Red Cross Food Section in appreciation of the weekly food parcels sent to each prisoner, and without which many would have died. All the 43 men who had been prisoners in Europe returned safely. Two of the 13 Far East prisoners died while in Japanese hands; as these prisoners had never been allowed to receive parcels, they were on their return given the value of the parcels in cash.

Throughout the war, *military personnel* were stationed in Stone, and private and public buildings were taken over, including Meaford Hall. Up to February 1941 the troops were entirely British; from then until March 1945 American troops were stationed in Stone, as well as at some of the hostels at Swynnerton. During this period it was estimated that half-a-million Americans passed through the town. American Red Cross workers were also billeted, and St. Joseph's Hall became a canteen under the title of *The Donut Dugout*. The American personnel helped in many ways with the life of the district, and Col. Raydar spoke of the kindness shown to them by the Stone people when a farewell party was given at Howard Hall on October 14th 1945.

In April 1943 the Admiralty commissioned property at Mill Meece as *H.M.S. Fledgeling*, for the training of Wrens in the maintenance of naval aircraft. By Christmas 1944 over 1500 Wrens had been successfully trained, and the ship then continued the same training for male ratings. From this changeover to the end of 1945, when training ceased, 160 Royal Navy, 420 Canadians, and 240 Dutch ratings had qualified as air mechanics. The establishment later became a police college.

The *Stone Red Cross* detachment, lapsed after the 1914-1918 war, was revived in 1942, and the *special Constabularly* which numbered 100 in 1939 was soon doubled. Stone's 17th (Staffs) Battalion of the *Home Guard* was one of the most enthusiastic, and its work reached a very high standard.

Throughout the war, Stone was playing a full part in the *industrial effort*. *Alvis Limited* of Coventry were working on the repair of Rolls-Royce aero-engines when their factory was blitzed. The firm took premises at Lotus (Stafford), at the old Glass works in Mill St., and in Joule's Brewery garages, and repair work was resumed. By December 1945 this new Alvis Division repaired 5,016 Kestrel and Merlin engines. The *English Electric Co.* took over the Cauldon works at Stone in May 1941 to make vital radio components. Personnel rose from 14 to 100 in 1942, and to 214 by 1943, while output rose to a peak figure of over 2,000 units a week. *Lotus Ltd. of Stone* diverted personnel in 1940 to the making of weathercovers for aircraft; then from early 1942 worked for six months on producing 10,000 dinghy packs. At the end of 1941 a small unit also produced electrical laminations, required for electrical motors in every branch of the services. In 1943 100 people were producing over three-quarters of a million 'slottings' each week, working in shifts from 6 a.m. until 11 p.m. *Henry Meadows Ltd.* of Wolverhampton used space at the Lotus Factory for the storage of thousands of components for Meteor engines, these coming under the dispersal arrangements for safe custody. Some 50 people were employed on the inspection and despatch of parts for the assembly of over 60 engines per week.

To aid workers in Stone, a *British Restaurant* was opened in the Market Hall in June 1943, with seating for 120 people, and continued until the end of 1945. Over a long period, well over 200 meals a day were being served.

The *Royal Ordnance Factory* built at Swynnerton resulted in the building of the Ministry of Supply estate at Walton. Work began in April 1941 and by August 1942 a group of building firms had built 220 houses, 220 flats and 40 staff houses. Many hundreds of workers were accommodated in the hostels near the factory, and huge numbers brought in by road and rail. At the time of peak production the Royal Ordnance Factory employed 5,086 men and 15,313 women. The railways, with reduced staff, got through a tremendous amount of work. At Stone station the number of passengers increased from 86,041 in 1938 to 124,182 in 1944, and in this latter year 50,000 troops travelled to and from Stone station on warrants. Goods traffic in 1945 was double that of 1938.

Industry demanded raw materials and everything usable had to be salvaged. In Stone the total value of *salvage* for war purposes was £3,400, besides 3,000 yards of iron railings, requisitioned for scrap metal. Over and above the need for materials was the need for money. Through *National Savings* between December 1939 and the end of 1945 a total of £1,940,555 was raised in the town.

Money for the Duke of Gloucester's Red Cross Fund, Prisoner of War Fund and Mrs. Churchill's Aid to Russia and many other causes was raised by the *farmers' and traders' efforts* to the tune of over £11,000, while the Red Cross Penny-a-Week Fund raised £2,638.

In August 1940 a local fund was started to raise £5,000 to buy a Spitfire for the R.A.F. This was achieved by October 1941, and the plane was named 'Star of Stone'; the plane formed part of one of the first Norwegian squadrons to be formed, and was flown by a pilot who had escaped from Norway with King Haakon. The plane was lost in 1942.

In money, in human energy and in nervous strain, the six years of war had tested the town of Stone as never before in its history. As in the previous world war the town had met every demand made upon it, and had every right to feel that this was a satisfactory ending to its long story.

NOTES AND REFERENCES

1. Staffordshire Chronicle, 2 January 1915.
2. For greater detail see Lieut. Walter Meakin's "The 5th North Staffords and the North Midland Territorials, 1914–1918."
3. Staffordshire Advertiser, 28 November 1914.
4. Staffordshire Chronicle, 5 June 1916.
5. ibid. 15 June 1918.
6. ibid. 24 January 1920.
7. Staffordshire Advertiser, 10 October 1914.
8. ibid. 7 November 1914.
9. ibid. 28 November 1914.
10. Their story has been told in the book, "The Irish Nuns of Ypres".
11. Staffordshire Chronicle, 30 March 1918.
12. Staffordshire Advertiser, 26 July 1919.
13. ibid. 15 January 1921.

POSTSCRIPT

It is too soon yet to assess the events of the last two and a half decades, and to see them in their true perspective. With a population now of 10,000, Stone appears to find itself once more at a crisis point in its history. We are surrounded by changes, sudden, widespread and often incomprehensible. We are beset by changes in education, in industry and in transport, whose meaning and value are alike not clear to us. Industries which were once part of Stone's life, Bent's Brewery and Cauldon Tiles, have gone as a result of mergers; Joule's Brewery appears to be going. New industries have come, such as Quickfit and Quartz and Doultons; one, Townson and Coxon, came and went again. Rumours and counter-rumours abound; the planners produce plans; the educationists produce theories; the Government proposes re-organisation of local government, so that Stone itself may soon cease to exist as a separate entity. Whether the spirit of Stone lives on will depend on its present and future citizens. The past will, it is hoped, never be forgotten. The story of this town's difficulties and successes over the years will, perhaps, be some encouragement in the uncertainty and doubts of these early seventies.